DEEP VALUE INVESTING

eBook edition

As a buyer of the print edition of *Deep Value Investing* you can download the eBook edition free of charge to read on an eReader, smartphone, tablet or computer. Simply go to:

ebooks.harriman-house.com/ deepvalueinvesting

Or point your smartphone at the QRC code here.

You can then register and download your free eBook.

Follow us on Twitter – **@harrimanhouse** – for the latest on new titles and special offers.

www.harriman-house.com

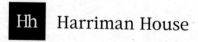 Harriman House

DEEP VALUE INVESTING

FINDING BARGAIN SHARES WITH BIG POTENTIAL

JEROEN BOS

FOREWORD BY MICHAEL VAN BIEMA

Hh

HARRIMAN HOUSE LTD

3A Penns Road

Petersfield

Hampshire

GU32 2EW

GREAT BRITAIN

Tel: +44 (0)1730 233870

Email: enquiries@harriman-house.com

Website: www.harriman-house.com

First published in Great Britain in 2013.

Copyright © Harriman House Ltd.

Author photo by Felix Bos.

The right of Jeroen Bos to be identified as the Author has been asserted in accordance with the Copyright, Designs and Patents Act 1988.

ISBN: 9780857192998

British Library Cataloguing in Publication Data

A CIP catalogue record for this book can be obtained from the British Library.

Hh Harriman House

This book is dedicated to my father

ABOUT THE AUTHOR

Dutch investor Jeroen G. Bos has lived in England since 1978. He has a diploma in Economics from Sussex University and has worked his entire career in the financial services industry, mainly in the City of London. He worked for many years at stockbrokers Panmure Gordon & Co, and it was here that his interest in value investing developed. This process accelerated after the October 1987 stock market crash, during which time he took inspiration from *The Intelligent Investor* by Benjamin Graham.

At the end of 2003 Jeroen joined Church House Investment Management to manage CH Deep Value (Bahamas), which in March 2012 became the UK regulated Deep Value Investments Fund.

He lives in Sussex, is married and has three sons.

Jeroen Bos holds investments in the Deep Value Investments Fund, Norcon Plc and Record Plc.

FOREWORD BY MICHAEL VAN BIEMA

MODERN FINANCE THEORY postulates a strong relationship between risk and return. Jeroen Bos and his investment style demonstrate the fallacy of this convenient but naive definition of the risk-return relationship. In this book, Jeroen explains how by being a deep value investor one weeds out investments that are both very low in risk and high in return

Jeroen practises a type of investing that I call Statue of Liberty investing – to paraphrase: *give us your poor, your forgotten, your unloved* … [1] The companies he looks into have for the most part either been forgotten by most of the investment community or are actively shunned by them. Lurking, however, in the recesses of this netherworld of the investment universe one finds some equities that represent the

---

1 A liberal rendition of the actual words that appear beneath that fine lady.

ultimate in value. These are equities whose value is not justified by the future earnings envisioned by the fantasy of management or analysts, but rather by the current facts as presented in the company's balance sheets.

Effectively, what Jeroen teaches us in this book is how to read and think about balance sheets in a simple and very effective way. His goal is to uncover companies and therefore investments where the assets on the balance sheet outnumber the company's liabilities in such a way that the 'risk' of investing in the company's equity is strongly mitigated, and, perhaps more importantly, can be accurately estimated relative to the potential return. The main focus of the book and of the 17 detailed investment examples it contains are so called net-net investments. These net-net investments were first described by Ben Graham who is widely considered the father of both value investing and, in fact, the field of security analysis. A net-net investment is equity where the current assets of the company outnumber all of the company's liabilities. As Graham put it, it is a way of buying a dollar for 50¢.

Jeroen began his value investing career as a broker in London where on his own he developed an attraction for both unloved securities and for 50¢ dollars. As he once told me, he had the ideal personality for this form of investing – being both stubborn and cheap. Joking aside, there is truth to his statement in the sense that great value investors have to both have a nose for cheap securities and then have to be incredibly disciplined in purchasing them only when they are really at value prices.

Jeroen later became a broker to Peter Cundill, the legendary Canadian value investor who generated north of a 17% return annualized over the course of his 33 years career. Peter was a personal friend of mine as well and a member of the board of advisors of my firm. While a kind and generous man, Peter was not a man to suffer fools and his profitable dealings with Jeroen, especially with Amstrad, are a testament to Jeroen's abilities to find investments of interest not just to mere mortals but to one of the super investors of the Graham school.

The book focuses on companies in the service sector since they are better able to rapidly adapt to changes in economic circumstance. Jeroen also stays away from companies that carry any significant amount of debt on their balance sheets, preferring instead to search for companies that are cash-rich.

The companies themselves span a broad cross-section of service industries, from a defense contractor to banking and currency exchange. Jeroen also describes some of his investments in retail and the difficulties associated with investing in that more 'fashion-driven' sector. Some of the investments described here can only be described as legendary. A number are so called three-baggers, but even some of the more modest successes are legendary in the sense that one can buy equity in companies at such large discounts to their value, as Jeroen puts it in the case of Morson group: "one could buy a profitable company with £500m in revenues for less than £20m".

The book is also complete in the sense that it provides a couple of examples of his mistakes and a few where the outcome is still uncertain. Perhaps the most instructive of this the Abbycrest case study, where Jeroen violates his own principle of staying away from companies with high levels of debt – unfortunately with disastrous results. Two other cases that provide fascinating reading are those of Barratt Developments and Gleeson, both British homebuilders and both of which worked out extremely well, but both of which had quite different risks despite being in the same industry.

Another unique aspect of the book is Jeroen's sell discipline. As he correctly points out, the types of investments he is looking for are not readily available in quantity. They are hard to find and frequently take a long time to 'develop'. Unlike many value investors, he does not necessarily sell when his investments reach fair value; rather, he waits till some earning momentum develops and pushes the share price higher. He, therefore, unlike many value investors, leaves less on the table.

One of the beauties of this type of investing, as pointed out, is that it does not depend on earnings estimates and forward-looking statements by management. These tend to be, not surprisingly, less reliable and far more volatile than the balance sheet. In fact, since most investors depend heavily, if not entirely, on these types of estimates, income statement investors create the price volatility of which Jeroen and other balance sheet investors are able to take advantage.

It takes a few characteristics to be a great value investor. Some of the things we look for at our firm are:

- a focus on the long term

- a willingness to take a contrary view

- patience

- discipline.

As you read through this book, think about how Jeroen and the investment cases he describes display these characteristics. It will serve you well in your own investment career.

Michael van Biema
New York, 2013

Michael van Biema is the former Columbia University finance professor and founder and managing partner of funds of fund group van Biema Value Partners, LLC, based in New York. He is the co-author of the book Value Investing from Graham to Buffett and Beyond.

PREFACE

THIS BOOK FOCUSES on a specific area of value investing, but it happens to be the area that has generated the biggest returns. Deep value investing is a defensive *and* high-potential strategy, picking out companies where it is very hard to lose money even in a worst-case scenario and where genuine potential means an almost unlimited upside when fortunes change. It is as simple as it is sophisticated. Above all, it is about standing apart from the crowd and letting the balance sheet do the talking.

This guide to successful deep value investing is aimed at those investors who are familiar with the stock market, enjoy the investment process, and are interested in generating better returns than the market in general – with a (much) lower risk profile.

It deals with UK-quoted companies, though its principles work equally well in any other country. Crucially, the deep value investing methods revealed here only rely on publicly available information. All the reader needs is an interest in finding investment opportunities that are off the beaten track but have a better-than-even chance of superior returns in the long run. Deep value investing means being happy to look at many different potential investments and choose only the most attractive ones amongst them. Patience is an important part of this process.

"All the reader needs is an interest in finding investment opportunities that are off the beaten track but have a better than even chance of superior returns in the long run."

I have written the book around a large number of investment case studies so as to make the content as practical and well-illustrated as possible. Amongst the success stories there are some investments which had disappointing returns and a few others where the investment has only recently been made. But there is, I believe, just as much to be learnt from these examples as from those where everything went smoothly.

In each chapter I give a short background to each individual company and how and when I found them. I then show exactly how I used publicly available information to build a clear investment case. Every chapter has a freely available online appendix (accessible via **www. harriman-house.com/deepvalueinvestingappendix**) where the public releases referred to in the chapter have been reproduced in their entirety. This is done so that the flow of the investment case is not buried in endless detail in the chapter, but all the information is there for those who want to take a closer look at what was available at the time.

This book is not meant to provide a mechanical investment approach that can be copied and forgotten. Rather, it aims to demonstrate an entire way of investing that can be adopted (and adapted) by any thoughtful private or professional investor: the logic of why it works, and the application of its principles and techniques to a wide range of real-world shares.

Like all investing styles, deep value investing is dependent on many factors and each individual investment tends to be unique in a number of ways. To quote the title of Richard Oldfield's excellent investment book, like all investing it is inescapably "Simple But Not Easy". Nevertheless, it is my hope that this book marks a significant step towards making this highly rewarding form of investing more accessible than it has ever been before.

Jeroen Bos
London, 2013

CONTENTS

INTRODUCTION: BEING A DEEP VALUE INVESTOR

WHAT YOU CAN GET OUT OF THIS BOOK

T HE AIM OF THIS book is to show, step by step, how to find those stocks that have the greatest potential to generate substantial returns. If you are looking to dramatically increase your odds of getting a much better return from equity investing then this book should be of interest.

The methodology described in this book will help you to identify stocks with great hidden potential. Take Chapter 13's Barratt Developments, for instance. At the time of being identified by the methods explained in this book (November 2011), this share traded at 90p. In May 2013 it was trading at 240p – an increase of 270% in under two years.

This book contains many examples of other companies whose shares have shown similar strong price developments – including Record Plc, ArmorGroup International, Harvard International and many more. More than this, it tells you how to find companies like this in future, before their prices explode.

After having read this book you too should be able to generate much better results from your stock market investments by identifying deep value shares at the right time.

FINDING FRIENDLESS COMPANIES

I first started to develop and apply the deep value methodology of this book in the autumn of 1987, after the Black Monday crash, when I worked as a stockbroker at Panmure Gordon & Co. in the City of London.

My early successes in applying this investing approach generated a dramatic and consistent hit rate, discovering great opportunities in companies like H. Young Holdings, Amstrad, Time Products and others. It would take some time before I managed my own fund at Church House, but meanwhile my results improved and I was able to learn how to avoid the kind of real clangers that damage overall investment returns.

My investment approach revolved around a way of analysing stocks differently to most people – I focused on criteria that the majority of equity investors ignored. Stocks I went after tended to have fallen off the radar, no longer had any analyst support, and usually boasted share price graphs that told a story of enduring disappointment. Their market capitalisation had now fallen and they had become pretty friendless. No one wanted them.

If I could identify solid companies within these kind of stocks ignored by 95% of the market, I had something unique to sell as a stockbroker. This was important because, like all stockbrokers, I was paid on commission.

TEAMING UP WITH A SUPER INVESTOR

But I also wanted to identify a potential group of investors to whom this investment methodology would be of interest. Enter Peter Cundill, a Canadian 'super investor'.

Peter, who unfortunately passed away in 2011, had founded the Cundill Value Fund in the 1970s, and since then had produced investment returns that left the stock market indices in his wake. He would invest on a global basis, usually going to those markets that had had the worst stock market returns that year, as they would have the "biggest bargains available".

I had come across the name of Peter Cundill on the shareholders' lists of many of the undervalued companies that I had found. Having identified Peter as a potential client, I now had to find a cheap company – but also one where his name did *not* appear on the shareholder list. Eventually I discovered such a stock and rang him out of the blue in his office in Vancouver, Canada.

The vast majority of people don't enjoy being cold-called, but I had prepared myself and was confident that I could interest him by mentioning this stock and a few salient points that illustrated its cheapness. Later that day I faxed him a simple spreadsheet on the company and shortly thereafter I was asked to buy this stock on his behalf. This continued with several other small capitalisation stocks until I identified Amstrad Plc in 1990.

A SWEET PICK

At that stage Amstrad was trading at a discount to its cash on the balance sheet, let alone its working capital position. In fact, Amstrad's shares were now trading at such a low level that we would theoretically be able to buy up the company, cease all its operations, pay off all the outstanding charges, and still be left with more cash than we had paid for the shares in the first place.

Amstrad had been floated in the 1980s by its founder Alan (later Lord) Sugar. The company had once been a stock market darling, but when I came across it in the summer of 1992 it had missed several earnings expectations and was something of a fallen angel. The outlook for the company was uncertain. The City was disenchanted with Amstrad and Alan Sugar. The price was exceptionally low. Sugar was at that stage still the largest shareholder in the company.

I rang Peter Cundill to tell him about Amstrad. Not long after this conversation, Peter decided to build a declarable position in the company, months before Alan Sugar attempted to buy the company back at 30p (a potential 50% return). Sugar's plans were voted down and the shares recovered, reaching a high of 146p in 1993 and 220p in 1994. The company was eventually taken over in 2007.

With his connections in the City, Peter was able to generate some media interest in his dealings in Amstrad and as a result got written up in a few newspaper articles at the time.

This was all well and good – my firm did the majority of the share-buying, and that was my reward for finding the investment opportunity. But it made me think for the first time that at some stage I would like to run an investment fund on these principles myself.

From there to me running the CH Deep Value Investments fund is a long story that we can cut short. It was my good fortune that a friend of mine, Mark Henderson, introduced me in 2003 to James Mahon, the CIO of Church House Investment Management. James, a good value investor himself, immediately grasped my approach to value investing.

He gave me the opportunity – and the rest, as they say, is history.

PART I. THE DEEP VALUE PHILOSOPHY

CHAPTER 1. DEEP VALUE INVESTING

A NEGLECTED METHOD

D EEP VALUE INVESTING has been around for a considerable amount of time, its investment results have been astonishing and still the majority of equity investors ignore its principles and follow a whole host of other approaches.

Why?

Deep value investing, at its simplest, is where assets are purchased at a deep discount to their real worth. This can require a good deal of patience. It takes time to find the right company, and it takes time for the company to come good.

So deep value investing is not conducive to buying no matter the investing climate. Nor is it about being a 'busy' investor. There is a whole advisory industry bound up with the stock market – firms and individuals whose main purpose is to advise clients on their investments. Unfortunately, this industry is structured in such a way that a lot of its income is generated on a transactional basis. This inevitably leads to a higher turnover of positions than is really justified – certainly than is conducive to a genuine value investing approach.

Investors are given wide access to opinion makers, surrounded by pundits' latest views and market calls, while companies are encouraged (even required) to update investors on an ever more frequent basis. Without necessarily realising it, investors' horizons are being constantly foreshortened. Short-term disappointments are seen as a reason to up and sell and look for better investments elsewhere.

This type of investment behaviour is closely associated with the market's fixation on earning prospects, now and in the near future. There is no escaping the commentary generated by the focus on these earnings. It gains wide coverage and inevitably influences share prices. Stocks get bought up till they reach levels where they are 'priced to perfection'; the slightest earnings disappointment is then punished with a weaker share price.

At the same time, other stocks get bought because they have underperformed others in the same sector and are therefore relatively cheaper. But this perceived value is not based on actual asset values.

Market noise like this drowns out actual facts. But this is also the deep value investor's opportunity: it means you can find hidden gems that everyone else has missed. In fact, you can find them just as everyone else is busily throwing them away.

BARGAIN ISSUES: TRUE DEEP VALUE

There are different kinds of value investing and not all are created equal. Seeking the stronger rewards of deep value investing means not settling for spurious value stocks.

After all, it is perfectly possible to find statistically cheap stocks that are nevertheless remarkably poor investments. Comparing a stock's price with its net asset value (NAV) is an important first step, but it does not tell you all that you need to know. A company's net assets may comfortably exceed its stock market capitalisation, but the nature of those assets can complicate things. Tweedy, Browne – a famous New York-based value investment company, workplace of Walter Schloss and broker to Benjamin Graham – found just this in its highly recommended study 'What has worked for us in investing' (**tinyurl. com/tweedybrowne**).

Many stocks merely trading at a discount to their NAV are undoubtedly cheap, but they often tend to be undoubtedly unexciting. They have gone through years of declining profitability, contracting markets and little hope of a sustained turnaround. Their balance sheets tend to be light on working capital but heavy on fixed assets, where a lot of value is locked up in (obsolete) plant and buildings. They often mention, in the notes to the accounts, that there is surplus land available for sale etc.

Statistically they are cheap. But, crucially, it is difficult to see how the gap between the net asset value and share price can be closed. Often in these cases the NAV eventually joins the share price as losses continue to accumulate and the margin of safety slowly but surely evaporates.

This is obviously not a type of value investing that is particularly attractive. The trouble with this type of discount-to-net-asset-value investing is that one invests in seemingly cheap stocks but they are actually not cheap at all. The nature of fixed assets, as the name implies, is that they tend to be illiquid and for that reason difficult to shift. Surplus land can be sold, for instance, but this can be quite a lengthy process, taking many years to complete, with many unknown obstacles along the way which could derail the whole process at any time. It is all very well that a lot of value seems to be there, but how can it benefit the investor?

And that is exactly why so many 'heavy fixed asset' stocks are, on the whole, not really good investments at all. Interestingly, Tweedy, Browne found that a more reliable indicator of an investment with potential is a share trading at a discount to its *working capital*.

BENJAMIN GRAHAM AND BARGAIN ISSUES

Assets, then, are all well and good – but *liquid* assets are what we're really interested in. The thinking of investing legend Benjamin Graham helps move us towards the full picture of what deep value investing involves.

In 1987, when world stock markets crashed and equity investing went through some very dark days, somebody mentioned to me that it was the ideal time to re-read Benjamin Graham's *The Intelligent Investor*. In fact, I hadn't yet read it for the first time, so I made a note to buy it. Once I started reading it, I knew I had found the fuller investing framework I had been looking for.

Having experimented on my own with value stocks, I could read balance sheets. But with the help of this book a whole new world opened up to me. I read the book in no time and have re-read it many times since. I find it particularly useful when the market goes through a difficult time and stocks don't react in ways that we expect – when everything is being sold off, the good and the bad, and the future of equity investing itself is being called into question.

It is actually at such a time that the value investor should be at his or her most active. However, it can be a pretty lonely place for the stock-buyer. *The Intelligent Investor* is a much-needed source of sanity and support in such moments. It continues to make perfect sense.

Benjamin Graham's classic really taught me *what* to look for in a balance sheet and how different assets affect the attractiveness of potential investments. The most attractive companies, according to Graham's results, are the so-called 'net-nets' or 'bargain stocks'.

The beauty with these value stocks is the prominence of their *current assets*. In the first instance, their fixed assets can be ignored completely. By prioritising shares with healthy current assets, you find shares whose value can be readily unlocked. Current assets are by their nature a lot more liquid and for that reason can be sold off quicker than almost any kind of fixed asset.

If we can find a stock whose current assets (i.e. inventories, receivables, cash etc.) minus its total liabilities are worth more than its current share price in the stock market, than we can talk of a stock that is trading at a discount to the net-net working capital position.

To put it a slightly different way, this is where the current assets minus current liabilities but also minus the long-term liabilities are *still greater* than the current market capitalisation. If that is the case, then we know on a statistical basis that we are dealing with a truly cheap stock. Even if it can never be sold off at a vastly improved share price, you still have a bargain on your hands. The assets are worth more than what you've paid for them.

The icing on the cake is that we have not taken into account any fixed assets. They effectively can be said to come free at the price paid.

These stocks are known as bargain issues. It is finding this kind of share that this book will focus on, as they consistently boast the highest returns. There are never that many. They can be elusive. They tend to appear, as Benjamin Graham nicely put it, "when Mr Market goes through one of his periodic depressive moods" – when stocks are being sold off with no regard to any underlying values.

But they are always out there; you just have to know where to find them.

CHAPTER 2. HOW DEEP VALUE INVESTING WORKS

IN THE PREVIOUS CHAPTER I gave some background to the philosophy of deep value investing. In this chapter I hope to lay out a detailed summary of how exactly it works and what it practically involves. It differs from most people's way of investing and it is important to get our heads around exactly how.

JUST THE FACTS

Firstly, deep value investing is much more concerned with the actual facts of a company than forward-looking announcements. This is because the former are largely based on reliable historic data, while the accuracy of the latter still has to be established. Deep value investing likes to deal with the facts as they exist. And it prefers to base all opinions on those facts.

Above all what we seek to establish is:

- What are the assets that we are now buying?

- Are they capable of generating attractive returns at some stage in the future?

After that, the emphasis is on buying assets at a discount; the future will (generally) take care of itself. Exits from value investments come in many forms. Indeed one attraction of this investment approach is the fact that when these assets are truly cheap they can obviously be made more productive in somebody's else's ownership. Hence it is not uncommon for deep value stocks to receive takeover approaches (as we will see in several chapters).

Of course, such approaches are often a mixed blessing. They speed the investment returns up, but I have often thought that we would have had better returns if the company had been left alone and we had waited for its eventual rehabilitation. Nevertheless, the possibility of takeover interest provides a safety valve of some sort. It is all very well to find these stocks; ultimately we have to rely on the market to do its magic on the share price, otherwise we end up with a collection of very cheap stocks no one wants.

ASSETS NOT EARNINGS

Deep value investing's focus on assets rather than earnings is no mistake. In this regard, deep value investing is significantly different to the majority of investing styles. What's the thinking behind this?

If you run your eye over all the different balance sheets of the companies featured later in this book you'll see something rather striking. It is true of almost all companies, in fact. The share prices of the companies tend to be very volatile, but the *net asset values* of these companies tend to be pretty stable.

Share prices oscillate around net asset values on a pretty regular basis because earnings are running the show. Companies go in and out of favour, earnings surprise either on the upside or disappoint on the downside, and share prices reflect these short-term reactions in either direction before resuming their long-term trends again.

It seems, then, that buying assets is a less volatile exercise than trying to predict the next level of expected earnings. After all, trying to predict earnings is a pretty complicated exercise. There are so many factors continuously at work that it doesn't take much to throw them off course. When expectations are high, a small disappointment can cause havoc.

In other words, we need to have a greater understanding of a company when we focus on the earnings. Happily, for deep value investors, this is not required when looking at assets.

CYCLICAL SERVICES SHARES

So what kind of shares are deep value investors interested in? What kind of assets matter? In the previous chapter we looked briefly at the problems with heavy fixed assets. Predictably, then, my favourite value stocks are those that are *light* on fixed assets and *heavy* on current assets. And these tend to be service companies – for example, recruitment firms, financial services, consultants, house-builders (from time to time) and so on.

Their price movements all tend to be quite cyclical (and, of course, earnings-driven), which means there will inevitably be opportunities to buy them cheaply at some point. Interestingly, cyclical stocks always look cheapest *on an earnings basis* (i.e. measured by their P/E level) at the top of their cycle and most expensive at the bottom of the cycle, when their P/E levels are sky-high as their earnings have collapsed. The beauty of this phenomenon for deep value investors is that exactly when they are most unattractive to the majority of investors is precisely when we want to be buying them.

When every earnings-obsessed investor is selling off service companies, the asset-interested investor is often presented with a number of attractive bargains. The outlook in the short term may indeed be terrible, but the nature of such service companies is that their business models tend to be pretty flexible. They are able to contract their operations before they really hit trouble, unlike (for example) manufacturers, who have far less flexibility: vast workforces, factories, supply chains etc.

These service companies can virtually survive with one man and his contact book, waiting for business to pick up and expanding as the economy starts to grow again. They tend to be very operationally focused. Any growth in revenue quickly falls down to the bottom line, pushing up (often exponentially) earnings per share. As a consequence, the shares will quickly respond to an improvement in business.

Indeed, big gains can be made even before any earnings recovery is apparent; the markets are often so relieved to see that the company is no longer expected to go out of business. Once earnings are re-established these shares can then travel a very long way.

A note on comparing stocks

An investing technique that often comes in handy for deep value investing is comparative analysis – simply looking at other companies within a sector once you've started looking in detail at your candidate. If you've got to grips with one firm in a sector you'll find checking out others is a lot quicker. And it can be very rewarding.

In the first place it is interesting to see where other shares are trading compared to their net asset valuations/net-net working capital levels. You may find other investment ideas hiding amongst them. It is also a very good exercise because you can see how companies in the same sector treat different balance sheet items. This can have a great influence on valuations, and if there is one amongst a group of companies that treats an item on its balance sheet completely differently to the others it is a very good reason to do some careful analysis. It usually means a share worth steering clear of.

By looking at different companies in this way one also quickly learns which management team is the more conservative and has positioned their company in order to deal best with periods of economic contraction.

Doing all this for balance sheets over a number of years means that the figures tell a story. The consistency (or lack thereof) of that story can tell you a lot more than figures in isolation. Indeed, if earnings are volatile in a sector or company, it is a much simpler way to get to a company's true worth. Start with balance sheet valuations and then look at income statements.

I realise that this is not the usual way investors approach potential investments. The typical approach is to start with the earnings and the earnings expectations – things easily manipulated, quite legally, and which can be subject to many influences (hence their volatility). It is very easy to get carried away with ever-rosier views of a particular company's future earnings prospects, and accept that you should pay up for this anticipated growth, no matter what the competition is up to or what new technologies may yet appear.

But it is not very good for an investor's bottom line.

HOLDING ON FOR THE RIDE

Once a share's price starts to really go up, I differ to many value investors. As the share starts rising on improved earnings, I effectively cease to be a value investor. Instead I become very interested in what the market's expectations are going forward. What do I mean by that?

Well, I will be selling into an earnings-driven market, and I want to sell at the point that maximises my profits.

Of course, if I have achieved the value investor's goal and bought a 'net-net' (or something close to it), where the company's current assets are worth more than their market capitalisation, I know that I have a margin of safety. This is why deep value investing is so important in a market crisis, when the immediate outlook is still pretty unclear. It's marvellously defensive as well as offensive. But that's not the same as maximising profits.

To sell these stocks when they hit their net asset value, as some value investors would insist, would mean that my upside might only be some 10% or so. But by waiting for the earnings to re-establish again, they can easily go up 100% or 200% (not at all uncommon).

Great deep value stocks are hard enough to find in the first place, and I am certainly not in the mood to let them go just when it starts to get interesting.

THE REST OF THE BOOK

So that is the thinking behind my style of deep value investing: swimming against the earnings obsessives to pluck out liquid-asset-rich companies with nimble service-focused business models. Then buying them when no one else will, and selling them when everyone else wants them.

These otherwise not particularly spectacular stocks can become spectacular when bought at the extremes of valuation. The rest of the book will illustrate, in detail, exactly how (and how not) to chase down such companies, by revealing the detail of a number of real-life investments I have made in this fashion.

Each chapter is dedicated to an individual stock. I will explain the investment cases for each and how they have behaved since we bought positions in them. As mentioned earlier, this is not a simple litany of success. That would be dishonest and less-than-helpful for the aspiring deep value investor, who must be as aware as any other that investment is never so simple. Hence two chapters are dedicated to so-called value traps: stocks that looked like good value investments, but turned out to be anything but attractive. And the last six chapters are devoted to low-priced stocks which I currently hold, and which I hope are ready – in due course – to become the next stock market stars.

PART II. DEEP VALUE SUCCESSES

CHAPTER 3. SPRING GROUP

Bought at: 22p (December 2008)

Sold at: 62p (October 2009)

RECRUITMENT COMPANIES ARE often ideal deep value candidates. They invariably have strong balance sheets and are highly operationally geared; profitability tends to bounce back on higher sales and better utilisation levels. On the other hand, when entering periods of contraction their share prices tend to be very vulnerable and can quickly fall to lower levels.

This was the case with Spring Group in 2008.

COMPANY BACKGROUND

When I first came across Spring Group in 2007 it was particularly strong at recruiting IT staff in the financial services sector – especially for banks. Profitability had fluctuated over previous years and the company had grown to some extent through acquisitions, a major one being the purchase of Glotel in 2007.

It had traded as high as 164p in 2004, but with the onset of the recession in 2008 the share price had fallen, even though the firm continued to trade profitably. The company was seen as something of a mixed bag, with several acquisitions that still had to be bedded down and profitability that lagged its recent corporate activity.

INVESTMENT CASE

The company released preliminary results on 28 February 2008 for the year ended 31 December 2007. These showed that revenues had grown strongly, helped by the acquisition of Glotel; net fee income had increased by 22%; and its gross margin had strengthened. Basic earnings per share were up by 22% to 3.76p.

The balance sheet showed current assets of £123,415,000, mainly trade receivables and cash. Total liabilities came to £75,245,000, so the net-net working capital position worked out at £48,170,000. With the number of shares outstanding at 159,079,935, the net-net working capital per share was 30.3p.

In early 2008 Spring Group's share price was still trading above these levels. But as explained in Part I, the service sector always attracts my attention: the shares are volatile but the companies' balance sheets tend to be much more stable. On top of that, they find it much easier to contract in crisis and revive quickly later on.

Spring Group's price had certainly proved volatile. The net-net of Spring Group at 31 December 2006 worked out at 34p, while the share price during 2007 had reached a high of 88p and a low of 44p. So while I waited for volatility to bring the share price lower, I needed to find out more about the quality of the company's assets.

Fortunately these service companies are very easy to analyse – with uncomplicated balance sheets – so this wasn't very difficult. In the case of Spring Group, for example, the net-net was (as said) around 30p. Adding the fixed assets to this, we got to a total net asset value per share of some 52p (i.e. £34,894,000).

And it was soon clear that this was not the whole story. Looking at the components of these fixed assets, we could see that property, plant and equipment came to only £2,579,000, goodwill and intangibles (remember the company had made several acquisitions in the past) came to £26,306,000 and there was a deferred tax asset of £6,009,000. In other words, goodwill and intangibles were *75% of fixed assets*.

In my calculations I generally ignore goodwill and intangibles as they are the most unreliable of assets. They tend to evaporate as a company encounters a more difficult business environment – loss of market share, for example, can put severe pressure on goodwill valuations. For that reason, the value investor is probably better off forgetting them, instead relying on the more durable assets. Goodwill certainly has a role to play, but it tends to be in those companies that display more stable and growing earnings, and these are unlikely to be potential targets for the value investor.

All this meant that while the net asset value of Spring Group looked like it was 52p, on closer inspection it seemed that it was really only 35p. This was not the end of the world – just something to bear in mind. Reassuringly, there was just 5p worth of fixed assets in the mix.

Spring Group's main assets seemed to be *trade and other receivables* and *cash and short-term deposits*. These were brilliantly liquid. But the next step was double-checking how valuable they really were.

It is very important, when evaluating trade and other receivables, to look at a company's clients. Who are they? Do they have a record of non-payment or doubtful debts? If a firm's clients are also struggling then it is sensible to expect that perhaps not all receivables will actually be received. This figure should then be discounted, perhaps quite aggressively. But in the case of Spring Group, the majority of the company's clients were major corporations in good financial health. That meant the valuation of this asset could be much closer to the stated amount.

It is also important to see how large a company's biggest client is and what they represent to total turnover, as well as to check client concentration. If the top four clients represent more than 75% of turnover then a company is in an uncomfortable position, especially when entering a recession. Luckily, again, none of these applied to Spring Group.

I now knew what I would pay for shares in Spring Group and was assured of its soundness as a business. It was just a matter of time to see if the share price would drift to lower levels than the net-net working capital position of 30p per share and become a genuine deep value investment.

OUTCOME

By waiting to buy companies at a discount to their net asset value – or, better still, buying at a discount to net-net working capital – we tend to join the party after most of the inevitable disappointments have been announced. Of course, there is still the chance that we can lose 100% of our investment, but the beauty of this investment style is that we should be now on the right side of the price paid and the value received. I am not saying that no further disappointments can be just round the corner, but typically we will be getting in close to the true value of the company.

And so it was in the case of Spring Group. We knew what we wanted to pay for it. We just had to wait to see if an opportunity arose for us to buy these shares at the price we wanted.

Fortunately this opportunity came along not long thereafter, when during a strong market sell-off the share came under great pressure and we were able to buy at 22p in late 2008. Less fortunately, having patiently waited for this moment, we never got the volume of stock that we had hoped for.

On 11 August 2009 the company announced a recommended cash offer by Adecco UK Holdco Limited (a wholly-owned subsidiary of Adecco S.A.). Under the terms of the offer, scheme shareholders would receive 62p in cash for each Spring Group share – a 182% return on our investment.

CHAPTER 4. MOSS BROS

Bought at: 27p (February 2011)

Sold at: 70p (March 2013)

MOSS BROS WAS not a classic net-net stock, but it did look very cheap after the firm pulled off one of the deals of the century. In the end that was enough to qualify it for a deep value investment.

COMPANY BACKGROUND

Moss Bros is the British suit specialist, selling and renting men's clothing online and through 155 retail stores in Britain and Ireland. The company is over 100 years old and has been listed on the London Stock Exchange since 1947. With the onset of the recession of 2008/9 the company's share price drifted lower and the business lost money in 2009 and 2010. Selling formal menswear in a recessionary environment may not have been the hottest prospect.

However, on 7 February 2011 Moss Bros released a trading update and a proposed disposal. It was only the day after this announcement had been made and written up on the front page of the second part of the *Financial Times*, that my colleague James Mahon mentioned it to me.

I read the article and then went back to the actual announcement that Moss Bros had made. What the company had announced was the following (underlines here and throughout the book added by me):

> "Moss Bros, the UK's number 1 branded suit specialist, today announces its intention to dispose of its 15 Hugo Boss franchised stores to Hugo Boss UK limited (the 'Purchaser') for <u>a cash consideration of £16.5 million</u>."

The full statement went on for a further five pages but this seemed interesting enough.

INVESTMENT CASE

The Moss Bros/Hugo Boss franchise had at that time another four years to run. It either had to be renegotiated, or the value would have gradually eroded to zero as the agreement drew to a natural close. To get such a big premium for 15 franchised stores (albeit ones which did trade profitably) was very interesting, to say the least. Somebody was in a hurry to get these back.

At that time Moss Bros had a market capitalisation of £25.5m and operated 155 retail stores. Subtract the fresh £16.5m of cash and the loss of the 15 stores from this and my basic thinking was that at the current price I could now effectively be buying a £25m Moss Bros Group for some £9m, and still have a store portfolio of 140 outlets.

Although the company had reported a loss for 2010, in the same statement released on 7 February it also announced:

"The transaction is integral to Moss Bros' recently developed strategy to focus growth and resources on the company's own brands.

"The Disposal will enable Moss Bros to significantly accelerate this strategy as the cash proceeds of the Disposal will provide funding for the redevelopment of the Moss-branded stores, investment in the service experience, piloting and an appropriate roll out of new initiatives such as Moss Bespoke, and the development of a customer relationship management system to leverage the value of the hire business."

It further confirmed,

"that it continued to trade well during the important Christmas trading period, and total sales and margins continue with a positive like-for-like trend. Like-for-like sales were up 7% for the 26 weeks to 29 January 2011, and up 9.1% for the 52 weeks to 29 January 2011. Gross margin also continues to perform well. The Board remains confident of the outturn for the full year."

This all read pretty well, I thought. It was interesting to see that on 7 and 8 February no transactions had taken place in the shares of the company. We bought them soon thereafter at 27p.

The price we paid was equal to the firm's net asset value. However, the net-net only worked out at 6.55p. But if we included the sale proceeds of the Hugo Boss franchise – highly liquid assets, with £4.2m of cash coming in on completion and the rest of the £16.5m in instalments by the end of the year – then the net asset value would, based on very rough calculations, work out at something like 45p.

A non-net-net value stock, then, but one which qualified as a deep value investment thanks to genuine richness of liquid assets and the potential to turnaround with a new strategy (and as witnessed by the value others placed on 15 of its stores).

OUTCOME

Around that time the second biggest formal hire company in the UK went out of business, undoubtedly good news for Moss Bros. This allowed it to immediately increase its hire prices in a very price-inelastic market.

Indeed Moss Bros became the dominant player in the formal hire business in the UK, a very attractive business for the company to be in, and this only augmented that. It has very high barriers to entry. It also means a certain amount of predictable recurring revenues. Most weddings happen during the summer months, for instance. Then there's the racing season based around Royal Ascot, the Grand National, the Derby and so on; not to mention increasingly popular leavers' 'proms' or balls at the end of the school summer term.

Management also began experimenting with designer labels, enabling the company to charge higher prices compared with its standard wear. What may have seemed like a pretty mature business at first sight still had plenty of opportunities like this for further tweaking.

Due to the strong cash position in the wake of the Hugo Boss deal, the company was in a very good position to negotiate with landlords, assuaging any concern about another retailer going under.

The store portfolio was in the process of being upgraded, not only moving to better locations but also helping to change the image of the group. Bespoke was introduced as an additional service offering, but also very much to enhance the company's image.

It seemed that the sale of the Hugo Boss franchise came at the right time for the company.

* * *

The share price did not immediately react to these positive developments. That would take some time – but it did happen.

On 30 March 2011 the company released preliminary results for the 52 weeks ended 29 January 2011. The company still announced pre-tax losses, but like-for-like retail sales were up 8.9%, while hire sales were up 10.9%.

Brian Brick, CEO, said:

"We have made good progress on all operational priorities we set out at the beginning of the year and this has had a very positive impact on trading, despite the difficult trading environment last year. We continue to build clear strategic goals, an effective management team and a track record of delivering. Current trade reflects strong like-for-like growth and our continued focus on the operational priorities, with the support of our strong balance sheet, gives me great confidence that we will fully achieve the potential for this business."

It seemed that the seeds had been sown and better things could now be expected.

This came with the half-yearly financial report released on 27 September 2011. The period it focused on showed the company returning to profitability and cash balances of £15m. Like-for-like sales continued to grow. Management spoke of its expectations that the full-year results would be ahead of previous management expectations.

These were positive comments for the company and the share price started to reflect them. Ever since, positive statements continued to be released and the price carried on rising. We eventually sold our position in March 2013 at 70p.

The company was undoubtedly moving in the right direction and returning to profitability, but it was clear that much of the share price rise was down to the perception of better times ahead. On a P/E basis it was getting very expensive, with the price above the NAV by a considerable margin. In other words, the share price was now trading at 'priced to perfection' levels and therefore vulnerable to possible setbacks. The perfect time to sell.

Moss Bros was a very unusual value stock. It had not previously appeared on any value screen. It looked an unlikely winner in a seemingly very unattractive market segment. This highlights the danger of looking at new investment opportunities with preconceived ideas. It is better to look at the figures and let them do the talking. When a company with market capitalisation of £25m sells a division for £16.5m in cash, it is saying something fairly loud and clear – what is remarkable is how few people were willing to listen until much later on.

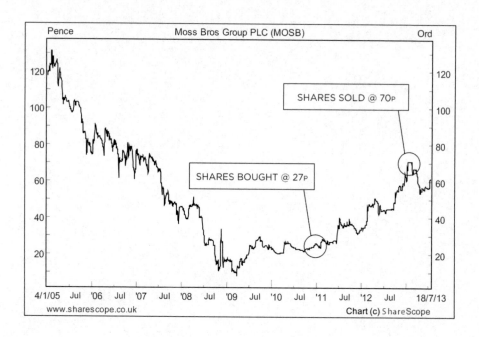

CHAPTER 5. ARMORGROUP INTERNATIONAL

Bought at: 27p (November 2007)

Sold at: 80p (March 2008)

I HAVE A LIST OF companies that look interesting but feel too richly priced to be considered as value investments. The advantage of keeping a list of potential investments like this is that I know what I want to buy and know what I am willing to pay. As investor Jim Slater often says: "When preparation and opportunity meet, good things can happen".

ArmorGroup International was once on this list, till events conspired to lower its price to true deep value territory.

COMPANY BACKGROUND

When I first came across ArmorGroup International in 2007 it was a rather unique services company quoted on the London Stock Exchange. This British firm had been around for 25 years and was recognised as a leading provider of defensive and protective security services to national governments, multinational corporations and international peace and security agencies operating in hostile environments. The company provided its clients with training, consultancy, security and mine action services. It employed 9,500 highly trained and experienced employees and operated in 38 countries. Over the past two years it had supported its clients in more than 100 countries across the Middle East, Africa, North and South America, the CIS and central Asia.

There were many big integrated providers in the services sector but none was really like ArmorGroup – they tended to concentrate on non-hostile environments, be it administrative services, recruitment etc. Globally there were a few similar companies, but they were usually US-based. This made it more difficult to compare to other companies in the sector for valuation purposes.

What had originally attracted me to this company was its business model. It was all based on long-term contracts that tended to run for four to five years, with firm pricing, in a global market that continued to show steady overall growth.

However, while the business characteristics of the company might have been attractive, companies dealing with conflicts never have a great standing in the market. And there was another twist: although headquartered in London, the company's main office was in the US. It all added up to the company never attracting a wide following.

The stock market performance of the company – first listed in 2005 – was not great, even if the price was too high for a value investment for a long time. The price peaked in 2005 at 273p but had steadily fallen and by November 2007 was down to 26p after a profit warning and the resignation of the CEO, David Seaton.

That's when I grew seriously interested in the company.

INVESTMENT CASE

In the profit warning ArmorGroup said that a number of contracts in Iraq had been "severely affected by the Blackwater incident" in Baghdad on 16 September, when 17 Iraqi civilians were shot dead by Blackwater military contractors and a further 20 were wounded. ArmorGroup also said that a significant contract had not "built up" as speedily or significantly as the client had projected.

The company further conceded that it continued to face "onerous administrative and human resource requirements" on a US Embassy contract in Afghanistan. The weak US dollar also continued to impact the firm.

The Baghdad incident mentioned here involved Blackwater, the US-based and quoted competitor to ArmorGroup. After this horrendous event, all of Blackwater's Iraqi operations were suspended. A much wider political discussion started over the role of these kinds of companies in Iraq and further afield. It was no great surprise that the share prices of such companies became very weak. There was a lot of uncertainty.

With all these doubts at work, I was still interested in ArmorGroup. My reasoning was that these companies were so embedded with their clients (i.e. national armed forces) that it would be very difficult to unwind such arrangements. What was more likely was the introduction of new regulations and restrictions. ArmorGroup's kind of business would continue to exist in one form or another.

When I had first become interested in ArmorGroup, I had been looking in detail at the results released on 19 September 2007 – the interim results for the six months ended 30 June 2007. In this document David Seaton, the CEO, had commented:

"We have achieved modest revenue growth in the first half with the Group's operations in Afghanistan and Nigeria contributing to an <u>overall revenue growth of 26% outside Iraq</u>. We have also seen <u>revenue growth</u> from both our training and mine action divisions, in line with our strategy of diversifying revenues away from protective security services. Market consolidation is gathering pace, giving rise to an increasing number of <u>acquisition opportunities</u> on which the Group is <u>well positioned</u> to capitalise and leverage its operational gearing.

"Consistent with prior years, the full year outcome will be heavily weighted towards the second half of the year as <u>significant new contracts</u> won in the first half, and those we continue to win in the second, <u>mobilise as expected</u>. The Group continues to have <u>a strong pipeline of identified opportunities</u> going forward with tenders awaiting award of $227 million (2006: $142 million) and the Board remains confident in the Group's prospects for the full year."

Some key points from these results were:

- revenues were up, at $137m ($134.4m in 2006), with non-Iraq revenue rising 26% to $80.5m

- an operating profit of $3.5m ($4.3m in 2006)

- a profit before tax of $2.5m ($3.7m in 2006)

- basic earnings per share of 3.5 cents (4.9 cents in 2006)

- strong cash flow from operations of $8.6m ($12.4m in 2006)

- net debt of $7.6m at the period end, compared to $3.6m at 31 December 2006

- unchanged interim dividend declared of 1.25 cents per share.

Up until the profit warning of 27 November 2007 the company had been profitable since joining the stock exchange in 2005. The balance sheet was in good shape.

We can see that the net-net working capital position on the balance sheet was $24,790,000. The number of shares in issue was 53.4m, giving a net-net per share of 46 cents. The dollar/sterling exchange rate at the time meant a net-net of 30p per share (the share price was then 27p). The company had tangible fixed assets in the form of property, plant and equipment of $30.2m. There were quite a few intangibles but these I tend to ignore when calculating net asset values. So we could argue that the net asset value was *at the very least twice the share price* of November 2007.

We bought into the company at 27p in November 2007.

OUTCOME

After we bought the shares not much happened. The price had found a new level at 27p. No real news came out and the company really operated in something of a vacuum. The Blackwater incident had disappeared from the front pages but its effects were still being felt.

On 20 March 2008 the company announced preliminary results but also that the board had reached agreement on the terms of a recommended cash offer for ArmorGroup by G4S Limited (a wholly owned subsidiary of G4S Plc).

The recommended cash offer was at a price of 80p per share – a 196% profit on our 27p purchase.

The decision to buy ArmorGroup may have looked like glorified gambling, but I would disagree. It was a service company with a very low valuation, an ideal candidate for my style of deep value investing. As mentioned, service companies have far greater flexibility when they go through adverse times. The business can be shrunk very dramatically in a short space of time; there is no need to close factories. Usually there are no legacy issues or onerous pension fund obligations: such companies tend to be too young to have such problems. Legal claims are, of course, a completely different issue – fortunately that was not a concern here.

It is interesting that ArmorGroup and Record (Chapter 17) both went through an extended period of their share price weakening over time. They then entered a twilight zone where further bad – not even devastating – news could cause great damage to the already weak share price. This is useful to bear in mind when following the kind of deep value investing approach I take. I tend to screen for companies by comparing their net asset value to their share price and don't worry too much about the immediate earnings outlook. This means I join the party after the share price has already disappointed many investors. Lots of them are ready to capitulate. Many feel rather embarrassed for still owning the stock. Experience suggests it will take only a nudge to tip them over the edge and make a share a true value investing bargain. It can be well worth waiting for that to happen.

Admittedly ArmorGroup may not have been your typical exciting-but-overlooked business. Nevertheless, at the price that we bought it we didn't really pay anything for the company at all. Add to that the fact that it was operating in growing markets with long-term contracts, and it was an appealing prospect. The results that ArmorGroup announced on that buyout day in March 2008 showed that revenues had grown by 8%, it had earnings per share of 5.5 cents, a strong operating cash flow of $25.3m (not bad when compared to its market cap) and it continued to pay a dividend. Although the G4S bid was welcome, without it we still would have owned part of a company that was certainly not dying on its feet.

As with my other deep value investments, I had found and bought a promising share by simply relying on everything the figures told me, especially when looking at several years of data. I have found this to be a lot more reliable than next year's profit expectations.

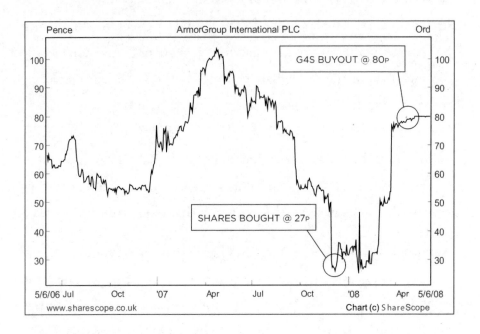

CHAPTER 6. MORSON GROUP

Bought at: 39p (April 2012)

Sold at: 50p (May 2012)

R ECRUITMENT COMPANY SPRING GROUP (Chapter 3) had a strong balance sheet, but not all value investments have to be able to boast this. Morson Group, for instance, had a far weaker balance sheet, with quite some debt. Nevertheless, it still made sense as a deep value investment.

COMPANY BACKGROUND

Morson Group – "the UK's leading provider of technical contracting personnel to the aerospace and defence, nuclear and power, rail and other technical industries" – was a recruitment company similar to Spring Group but with a focus on different sectors. The company was listed on the London Stock Exchange's AIM market on 30 March 2006, at an issue price of 160p, giving the group a market capitalisation of £72.5m.

In 2008 the shares reached a high of 196p but had steadily declined since then, reaching a low of 39p in March 2012. The group had remained profitable since listing in 2006. Profitability had, however, declined from a high in 2007, when pre-tax profits were £10.1m, to an expected pre-tax profit in 2012 of £6.5m.

INVESTMENT CASE

A good way of finding potential value investments is regularly checking the new lists of 52-week lows. This was how I found Morson, trading at 39p – a new low for the year. The stock looked to be very cheap to me. Although the company's profitability had clearly declined over the past few years it was still profitable and was expected to generate earnings per share of 10p, implying that the stock was trading on a price earnings level (P/E) of less than four-times – very low. It had sales in 2011 of £508m and a market capitalisation of only £18m. On these two factors, the stock looked to be reasonably cheap, but at this stage it was not yet established whether it was cheap on a balance sheet valuation.

Unfortunately the balance sheet of Morson Group was not so good. It carried quite a bit of debt. On 30 March 2012, Morson Group issued audited preliminary results for the year ended 31 December 2011. These showed that the group had increased revenues by 11% to £507m, but pre-tax profits had fallen by 38% to £5.7m (which still left earnings per share at 10p). So, not great but still profitable.

The company had highlighted the margin pressure and this was clearly something that the market worried about. Morson also announced that major contracts were up for review and had to be tendered for (representing some 30% of group turnover), spelling further uncertainty for the group's immediate outlook.

However, in the statement under the section 'Outlook', after stressing its careful approach to difficult times, the firm revealed that:

> "there are <u>significant medium to longer term opportunities</u> for the group with HS2 and other major rail infrastructure improvement works, aircraft carriers, weight-driven civil aerospace projects and of course nuclear energy delivery amongst many other projects. Engineers are a sought after global resource and <u>we look forward to, and are proud to be part of, the delivery of the future infrastructure and technology programmes that will ensue</u>. We have experienced management, have attracted additional staff to support our goals and approach the future and meeting these challenges with confidence."

The company obviously faced uncertainty – but the industry sectors that it supplied were not going to disappear, nor were contracts about to dry up.

Turning now to the consolidated balance sheet in these results, as at 31 December 2011 we see the following:

CURRENT ASSETS	£
Trade and other receivables	93,448,000
Cash and cash equivalents	2,636,000
TOTAL CURRENT ASSETS	96,084,000

But against these current assets it had the following:

CURRENT LIABILITIES	£
Trade and other payables	(39,985,000)
Current tax liabilities	(258,000)
Obligations under finance leases	(57,000)
Bank overdrafts	(35,923,000)
Derivative financial instruments	(391,000)
TOTAL CURRENT LIABILITIES	(75,614,000)

The group had no further liabilities or long-term liabilities outstanding. This left the net-net working capital position at £20,470,000. The group had a total of 45,387,665 shares outstanding at that time, which meant that the net-net working capital position per share was 45p against a share price at the time of 39p. It was clearly a net-net stock. But it had issues.

In fact, most net-net stocks have their problems – it is rare (even something of a contradiction) to find the *perfect* deep value bargain. Significantly, the firm's overdraft position was clearly large in the context of its total liabilities.

A large overdraft is usually something that I am wary about, not simply in relation to a firm's NAV. An overdraft position is never as secure as a fixed-term loan. The overdraft maybe callable by the bank, putting a company in a very difficult position. Reliance on overdrafts is not rare when credit availability is poor, but that doesn't make me feel any more relaxed about it.

Fortunately under point eight in the same results, below the heading 'Borrowings', there was some encouragement:

"At 31 December 2011, the Group had available £14,952,000 (2010: £22,694,000) of undrawn committed borrowing facilities in respect of which all conditions precedent had been met."

This gave me some confidence that the group still had some leeway if the worst came to the worst. It was not a great position to be in. The fixed assets came to £39.6m, of which £33.3m was goodwill – definitely something to bear in mind. However, it was not an unusual position. Spring Group's fixed assets had a similar goodwill component.

With all the issues surrounding the group, we still decided to buy the shares. They were cheap, the firm was profitable and its revenues were pretty high in relation to its market capitalisation. It would not take much for management to turn the company around (or for an outsider to do it for them by buying it). *Ultimately, at 39p, you could buy a profitable company with £500m of revenues for less than £20m.* A final encouragement was that the owners of the company had a very large shareholding (40%), which should have helped them concentrate on the well-being of the company (or selling at a strong price).

Looking at it this way, it did not seem a lot of money at all. So we bought some shares at 39p and waited to see if they would settle at a lower level (in which case we would buy more).

OUTCOME

Shortly after we bought our shares the company announced that a new shareholder had bought a declarable stake in the company. The new shareholder managed an unquoted service provider very similar to Morson Group, and the share price perked up on this news as it could potentially herald a bid for the company from the same shareholder.

But it never came to that. On 25 May 2012, the company announced a recommended cash offer by MMGG Acquisition for Morson Group, at a price of 50p per share.

The Morson family had decided to take the company private again, arguing that the weakness of the share price had defeated one of the core reasons for its IPO – namely to attract and motivate good quality staff by offering them share options. It also mentioned that the share price weakness had weakened Morson's competitive position in the bidding for contract renewals.

It had been a profitable investment – not a great one, but in a few months we had gained 28%. If only all disappointing investments worked out so well!

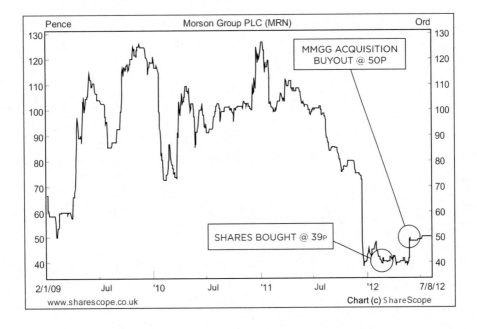

CHAPTER 7. HARVARD INTERNATIONAL

Bought at: 26p (August 2011) and 36p (April 2012)

Sold at: 45p (April 2012)

S HARES CAN LEAD A lonely life on stock exchanges. If they disappoint investors, they are soon overlooked, even forgotten altogether. Analyst coverage dries up as the share price dwindles – when a share becomes small and unloved it no longer pays to produce such material. But this also means that opportunities are created for value investors. Amongst this group of stocks some great value buys are always hidden.

It is amazing to consider that stocks can be found which are worth less than the cash on their balance sheet. But they most definitely can. By buying them you are purchasing cash at a discount – like paying £20 for a £50 note. You can purchase the whole company, using the cash in the balance sheet to do so, and have the rest for free.

Buying at a discount to cash doesn't really happen in the private market; the owners of private businesses know the value of their firms. Quoted companies don't have this protection. Their owners are shareholders who often have *no* idea about the true value of their companies, and are regularly ruled by a herd-like mentality.

Step in the value investor. The greatest chance of finding cast-iron value stocks is often amongst this group of unloved, mispriced shares, languishing down amongst the smaller market cap stocks (most often after a long tumble). This chapter deals with one of them: Harvard International.

Trading volumes in these minnows will be very low, so the buying and selling of these kind of stocks can be quite difficult. It may well mean that positions can only be built up over long periods of time. These stocks are a million miles away from the very liquid stocks of the FTSE 100 et al. But if they are cheap we should still look at them. And so it was with Harvard International.

COMPANY BACKGROUND

Harvard International is a distributor of consumer electrical goods in the UK and Australia. When I first started looking at them in 2010, the company had been a somewhat lacklustre performer on the London Stock Exchange, marginally profitable over the last few years but not making a lot of headway. As a result of this, management had instigated a programme to bring more focus to the company.

In August 2011, the shares in Harvard International traded at 26p – a new low – and I looked at them again.

INVESTMENT CASE

On 5 July 2011 the company had released preliminary unaudited results for the year ended 31 March 2011. These showed that revenues were under pressure due to a difficult British retail market, but it had made a marginal pre-tax profit.

In the release headlines Harvard also stated that it had net cash of £16m on the balance sheet as at 30 June 2011. Not bad for a company with a market capitalisation of only £13m.

The consolidated statement of the financial position showed the following:

CURRENT ASSETS	£
Inventories	7,200,000
Trade receivables and other receivables	13,000,000
Cash and cash equivalents	13,500,000
TOTAL CURRENT ASSETS	33,700,000

And the liabilities worked out as follows:

CURRENT LIABILITIES	£
Trade and other payables	(13,700,000)
Income tax payable	(400,000)
Provisions	(500,000)

There were no long-term liabilities so the total liabilities worked out as £14,600,000.

The net-net working capital position worked out at £19,100,000.

This was an extremely strong and liquid balance sheet. The cash position at 30 June, as said, was bigger than the market capitalisation. With the net-net working out at £19.1m and the number of shares at 51,284,858, the net-net per share was at 37p. Trading at 26p, this was obviously a very cheap share. So we bought the shares in August 2011 at 26p.

OUTCOME

Harvard International was working on some new products and had won a contract to supply set-top boxes to enable the consumer switch over to digital broadcasting, but it continued to be impacted by weak consumer demand in the British and Australian markets it operated in.

Still, I thought that the company was a good enough prospect to get a meaningful exposure to it, especially with its large cash position, promising new products and absence of losses. Before taking this further step I wanted to meet with the management to get a better feel for the company. It was certainly not held in high regard by the market, and there was comparatively little information available about the company (bar the results releases).

But when I rang the company to arrange a meeting it came up with lots of reasons why this would be difficult to arrange. Its corporate broker even called me to see what the purpose of the meeting could be. Normally, management reluctance to meet shareholders is a very negative signal.

It is possible to find management teams who are perfectly happy with the state of affairs in their dying company, and wish to leave the company to decline over a number of years – drawing their salaries all the while, burning through the capital of shareholders. As a general rule it is a comforting sign when companies like these have some institutional shareholders of note who can engage with management and stand up for shareholders' rights. This was certainly not the case with Harvard International.

However, there was a different reason for their reluctance to meet. And it wasn't bad. The company was about to release a statement regarding a possible offer.

The potential acquirer was Geeya Technology (Hong Kong), a wholly owned subsidiary of Chengdu Geeya Technology.

This was not as straightforward a bid approach as we were used to. Geeya was a Chinese company and it had to get clearances from several state and regional authorities in China before it could proceed with any bid for Harvard International. The price that Geeya mentioned in this release was 45p per share in cash, but there were uncertainties surrounding this.

At least the share price jumped up at the news – though still at a discount to the potential bid price, reflecting the risk that a bid would not materialise – initially settling at 40p.

Extension announcements (allowing Geeya to continue with its bid for Harvard while awaiting clearance from the Chinese authorities) were released on 26 October, 23 November, 21 December, 18 January 2012, 15 February, 14 March, 30 March and 5 April.

By this time the share price had started to weaken. The risk was really growing that a bid would not be forthcoming. Things had been dragging on.

Some shares became available at 36p in April. We were happy to buy as it was now trading again at a discount to the net-net working capital position. Buyout bid or no bid, if something is cheap, we like to buy to it.

On 13 April 2012, after a very long wait, Geeya finally announced that it was now in a position to make a recommended cash offer for Harvard International at 45p cash. This gave us a 73% and 25% profit on our two purchases.

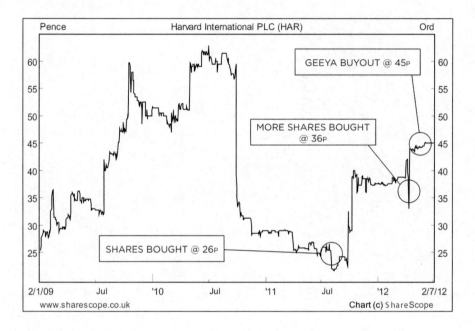

CHAPTER 8. VELOSI

Bought at: 82p (December 2009)

Sold at: 165p (December 2010)

COMPANY BACKGROUND

VELOSI WAS A VERY interesting company that was only listed on the London Stock Exchange AIM market in 2006, as part of the oil equipment, services and distributors sector.

It was a provider of asset integrity, quality assurance, quality control, engineering and HSE services to major national and multinational oil and gas companies. As I understood it Velosi would check oil rigs on an annual basis to see if they were 'fit for purpose'.

This created a recurring revenue stream – always good news. Meanwhile ever-increasing health and safety legislation meant an ever-increasing market for Velosi. The company was also in a very fortunate position in that it had few competitors capable of supplying these services on a truly global basis. Oil companies had to be able to have their oil rigs signed off on a particular date, even when based all around the world.

I thought that this was an interesting business model. I liked it a lot. The market had largely overlooked the company, and although its corporate head office was in the UK, management was based outside the country. The company was originally created in Malaysia and had mainly Malaysian management. Non-UK companies listed on the London Stock Exchange can often lead lonely lives like this, with little analyst coverage and a shareholder list that is light on British institutions. It then takes but a little for these companies to drop off the radar, even with attractive business models.

And so it was with Velosi.

INVESTMENT CASE

I spotted the company during the summer of 2009 as it looked pretty cheap on an earnings basis but was still trading (at 125p) on a premium to net asset value. The company released interim results on 21 September 2009 for the six months ended 30 June 2009. Highlights included:

- continuing track record of significant growth

- turnover for the first six months up 15%

- profit before tax up 10.4%

- earnings per share up 8.2% to 11.2 cents (6.9p); the previous financial year the EPS was 21.7 cents for the whole year

- net cash had grown to US$19.7m

- a steady flow of new contract wins coupled with 100% retention of existing contracts underpinned good visibility on future revenues.

The chairman commented:

> "Velosi has again delivered a good set of results despite the more challenging market environment. Based on historic trading patterns, revenues tend to be stronger in the second half of the year and, together with the excellent visibility provided by contract revenues, [this] gives us confidence that we will achieve a good result for the current year. Despite the weakening commercial environment, the company's strong underlying operating performance has allowed us to strengthen our financial position. As a result the company has a strong balance sheet with net cash of $19.7m million, remains cash-generative and continues to increase both revenues and profitability."

This all looked very good. To find a value stock with these characteristics is very unusual. Growing revenues, growing profitability and growing cash balances – this is a company that is actually expanding strongly rather than one that is drifting towards the value sphere.

As far as I could see, its lowly price was simply explained by the fact that, due to its 'unusual' background, it did not attract a following in London. I looked for anything else and failed to find it.

Deep value investors like to buy stocks at the greatest margin of safety.

We like to buy when the discount to NAV is at its greatest – better still at a discount to net working capital. (The net-net position.) This was possible for many of the investments in this book. But it's not – at least for me – an absolute cast-iron rule. Buying at a discount to net-net is buying the biggest margin of safety – we want the balance sheet to protect the investment against possible operating losses going forward. This means that I actually feel quite comfortable buying shares at the NAV level when a company is marginally profitable and the downside risk is more manageable. There is less to defend the investment against.

Evaluating just what the downsides might be – and their scale – is a tricky game. It's perhaps the one area in deep value investing where we can't just let the figures do the talking: the balance sheet, after all, deals with the past. Positive forward-looking statements aren't enough to base an investment on, but negative or cautious ones can be worth paying attention to when deciding just how much of a discount you need before the investment is safe inside value territory.

It is never straightforward and every case has to be approached on its own merits. There are no real certainties. It is the total picture that we are looking at to help us decide if something is worthwhile or a value trap. It takes a bit of experience – looking at lots of them over time will help you.

I have digressed somewhat, but it is important to explain that when the possibility exists that we are able to buy a company at NAV that is growing strongly, and is expected to do so for a considerable period of time, we value investors should have a look.

Making such a decision used a bit more information from the balance sheet than my other investments. The balance sheet of Velosi on 30 June 2009 looked like this:

ASSETS	$000s
NON-CURRENT ASSETS	
Goodwill	8,646
Other intangible assets	1,598
Property, plant and equipment	9,314
Investment in associated companies	1,364
Deferred tax assets	450
CURRENT	
Cash and cash equivalents	22,445
Inventories	4,048
Trade and other receivables	60,322
Tax recoverable	85
TOTAL ASSETS	108,304

LIABILITIES	$000s
CURRENT LIABILITIES	
Trade and other payables	28,166
Bank and other borrowings	2,824
Current tax liabilities	2,493
Deferred consideration	1,260
NON-CURRENT LIABILITIES	
Deferred tax liabilities	36
Bank and other borrowings	1,536
Other non-current liabilities	1,005
TOTAL LIABILITIES	37,315

The net working capital position was $49.6m. Shares outstanding of 47,765,871 gave a net-net per share of 65p at then-exchange rates.

If we look at the non-current assets (i.e. the fixed assets) we see that Velosi had $9.3m in property, plant and equipment and 'Other investments' of $1.3m, stretching to a NAV of $60.3m or $1.26 per share – about 79p.

We were able to buy shares in December 2009 at 82p, a slight premium to the NAV, but felt confident that this stock had the right characteristics and would continue to grow going forward.

OUTCOME

On 14 April 2010 Velosi released preliminary results for the year ended 31 December 2009. Highlights included:

- revenue steady at $183m

- operating profit up by 2.7%

- profit on ordinary activities before tax up 13%

- EPS up 5.1% to 22.8 cents per share (14p per share).

The chairman commented:

"To report a 13% increase in profitability, during a year when market conditions have been extremely challenging, is a very credible performance. Reported revenue for the group was stable in 2009 when compared to last year. However, excluding Nigeria which had to operate under exceptional circumstances, revenues actually increased by approximately 6.8%. This was achieved in a year in which oil prices dropped to around $40 per barrel, resulting in many oil companies reducing their expenditure.

"Looking ahead, we are seeing signs of recovery in activities alongside a higher and more stable oil price, with specific regions and countries experiencing an increase in investment in oil and gas infrastructure projects, although the overall mood in the industry remains cautious. Velosi has a strong order book which provides good visibility on future income and while we do not anticipate significantly improved market conditions, we expect to deliver a performance in 2010."

This was all reasonably encouraging. Although the share price had moved only a little higher I was happy to have 'paid up' – my confidence in the company seemed justified. The shares were trading on a sub-10 P/E.

Once I buy shares in a company, I read all subsequent release statements carefully. In the case of loss-making companies I check that my margin of safety is not melting away. If prospects change for the worse, I do not hesitate to sell and close my position.

In the case of Velosi the balance sheet was certainly not deteriorating. Indeed the company started to pay dividends. I was happy to hold this stock well into the future, not really having decided at what price I would sell them.

That decision was taken for me on 9 December 2010, with the arrival of a recommended cash offer by Azul Holding 2 S.A.R.L. to acquire the entire issued and to-be issued ordinary share capital of Velosi.

The offer price was 165p, a premium of 61.8p to the previous day's closing price, and a profit for us of 101%.

Velosi had been a relatively small and overlooked company, but in the disastrous wake of BP's failed deepwater well in the Gulf of Mexico in 2010 a business like Velosi was always going to see a pick-up in activity. The consortium that bought Velosi had wide experience in this field and were backed by the Carlyle Group and its partners.

Velosi proved to be a good investment. It was a very attractive business, trading at a very low price earnings level, with growing cash balances and confidence of further opportunities in the years to come. We could buy it at an attractive price because it was not really followed in the stock market. Based overseas, with little or no research coverage, and a shareholder list that had no major British institutions on it, it was left on its own – the definition of 'under the radar' in the financial world. There are shares like this in almost every sector.

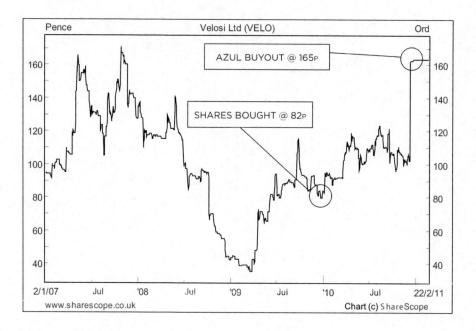

CHAPTER 9. B.P. MARSH & PARTNERS

Bought at: 87p (August 2012)

Sold at: 130p (April 2013)

B.P. MARSH & PARTNERS WAS a financial services company that had slipped under the radar, a bit like oil-rig services company Velosi (Chapter 8). The company is a niche financial venture capital provider. These are usually of no real interest to me due to the illiquidity of their underlying investments and the manner in which valuations are established.

But B.P. Marsh & Partners was slightly different.

COMPANY BACKGROUND

The company is part of the financial services sector and has been listed on the London Stock Exchange AIM market since 2006.

In 2012 I spotted the company on a list of companies that were trading at large discounts to their net asset valuations. Checking lists like this is a regular exercise for me – it's a good way of finding new potential investments. At a discount of over 50% to the NAV it looked cheap so I had to take a closer look at it.

If Velosi offers one kind of slightly unusual value investment (bought at a slight premium to NAV), B.P. Marsh & Partners represents another less usual kind. In order to explain why we bought the shares we have to go slightly away from the net-net working capital position and take a different look at the balance sheet. Hopefully it will become very clear.

INVESTMENT CASE

The latest report released by the company was the final results from 30 May 2012. Highlights included:

- net asset value up 7.8%

- net asset value per share of 171p (2011: 159p)

- share price trading at 48.2% discount to net asset value (as at 28 May 2012)

- consolidated profit after tax up 40.3%

- dividend of 1p per share declared

- annual compound growth rate of 12%.

The most important point in the chairman's statement, for me, concerned the shares the company held in Hyperion. This was the largest holding in the firm's portfolio. B.P. Marsh had recently sold some at 380p. This was an actual cash price at which a transaction had happened and for which cash had been received. Not IOUs or an exchange for other shares – real cash. This was encouraging; it increased my confidence in the portfolio valuations on the balance sheet.

It is important to show the company's investments as they were described in its statements. For the purposes of space – and because it was by far their biggest holding – I will focus on this investment in Hyperion.

The group first invested in Hyperion in 1994. Amongst other things, Hyperion owned an insurance broker specialising in directors and officers ('D&O') and professional indemnity ('PI') insurance. A subsidiary of Hyperion became a registered Lloyd's insurance broker. In 1998 Hyperion set up an insurance managing general agency specialising in developing D&O and PI business in Europe.

Here are the details of B.P. Marsh's investment in the firm:

B.P. Marsh's investment in Hyperion (March 2012)

Date of investment: November 1994

Equity: 19.4%, although this could dilute down to 18.3% with the group retaining an economic interest of approximately 19.2% post-dilution. (N.B. Following the partial disposal of shares the current equity holding of B.P. Marsh is 16.19%, which could dilute down to 15.63%, although B.P. Marsh would retain an economic interest of approximately 16.4%.)

31 January 2012 valuation: £33,888,000.

It is important to note that B.P. Marsh & Partners shares were trading at 87p in August 2012. With 29.2m shares outstanding, the total market capitalisation of the group was £25.3m. In other words, *it could be bought at a substantial discount to its largest holding.* (A holding whose valuation we could be confident in due to the partial sale of shares for cash to a unconnected party.)

B.P. Marsh & Partners was starting to look interesting.

The balance sheet of 31 January 2012, meanwhile, looked like this:

ASSETS	£000s
NON-CURRENT ASSETS	
Property, plant and equipment	14
Investments	50,624
Loans and receivables	5,983
CURRENT ASSETS	
Trade and other receivables	2,093
Cash and cash equivalents	666
TOTAL ASSETS	59,380

LIABILITIES	£000s
NON-CURRENT LIABILITIES	
Loans and other payables	(1,250)
Carried interest provision	(299)
Deferred tax liabilities	(7,415)

CURRENT LIABILITIES	
Trade and other payables	(295)
TOTAL LIABILITIES	(9,259)

The B.P. Marsh & Partners net-net working capital position in this case was a negative £6.5m, so it clearly wasn't a net-net bargain. But looking at the non-current assets, the investments – which included the investment in Hyperion at £33.8m – made things a lot more attractive. The fact that B.P. Marsh was able to create liquidity by partially selling down the Hyperion investment gave us a lot of comfort. The other investments came to a further £16.8m, and were all at different stages of development, but should have at least had *some* value. The statement described each investment individually. It would be too much to go through each one here. The fact that the Hyperion stake was worth some 30% more than the whole of B.P. Marsh & Partners was enough for us.

We had a margin of safety. The company was profitable and carried hardly any debt. So we bought in at 87p in August 2012.

OUTCOME

On 27 March 2013 the company released an announcement regarding 'Partial disposal of the Hyperion investment and trading update'. The company would receive a £29.2m cash consideration for the partial disposal of its remaining holding in Hyperion.

As we had bought in on the strength of this holding, we sold our shares in B.P. Marsh & Partners in April 2013 at 130p (a 49% profit). Although the NAV was still materially higher than the-then share price, I felt that the rest of the portfolio would take some time to mature. The main event had been the Hyperion investment.

It always surprises me what you find when looking for stocks trading at large discounts to their net asset value. Of course, lots of these companies have issues and it is difficult as an outsider to judge whether they can be turned around in order to close that NAV gap after you've bought in. But you can find other interesting companies like B.P. Marsh & Partners, where the matter is rather easier to judge.

Once found, it may still take some time before they start to perform positively. Patience is a double-virtue in value investing. After buying in it is simply a question of checking their balance sheets, watching for big losses (small losses are okay), keeping an ear out for anything positive in company releases or in the sector at large – and waiting.

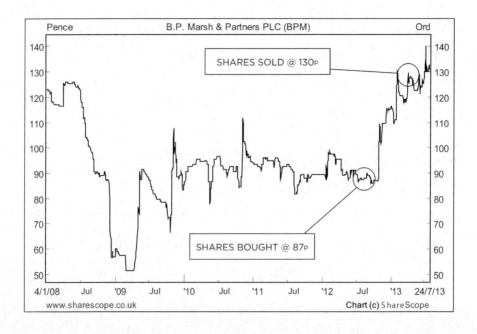

PART III. DEEP VALUE FAILURES

CHAPTER 10. RAB CAPITAL

Bought at: 13p (November 2010)

Sold at: 10p (June 2011)

T HIS IS THE FIRST OF two investments featured in this book which, for varying reasons, did not work out. I'll reveal my thinking behind the investments – and what can (hopefully) be learnt from them. After all, as investors we must try to learn as much from our mistakes as our successes.

COMPANY BACKGROUND

RAB Capital was a hedge fund manager that had been very successful in the early 2000s but came unstuck in the close of the decade with some bad calls – among them an investment in British bank Northern Rock.

The company was founded in 1999 and had very strong investment returns up to the end of 2007. It was best known for its Special Situations Fund, which since its inception in 2003 had generated very strong returns, putting it amongst the most successful hedge funds in the world. At one stage it held as much as $3bn in assets.

Problems started to appear in 2008 when the mood in the stock market turned negative, especially towards shares of banks and financial services companies. At that time RAB's Special Situations Fund had a position in troubled lender Northern Rock. At 5% of the fund, this was not overly large in itself. After all, RAB Capital had generated fantastic returns in the past by making big calls.

But there was an added complication this time. The media was focusing daily on the parlous state of the British banking sector, and in particular on Northern Rock. It became too much, unsettling investors in the Special Situations Fund. What started as a trickle in redemptions from the fund soon turned into a torrent of redemption requests.

On top of this, RAB Capital was a quoted company itself. This was certainly no great help at this stage. RAB Capital had to update the market about its funds on a regular basis. Soon it was making public the number of redemption requests.

Most hedge funds are private companies – i.e. not quoted – which allows them to operate far away from the public gaze. They don't have to disclose the wellbeing or otherwise of the funds that they manage. Stresses in their funds are known only to a few people. Difficulties can be dealt with privately. This was not a luxury that RAB Capital had. Instead, forced to provide a virtual running update on its funds, news of problems and redemptions encouraged further redemptions. Liquid investments were sold to satisfy these requests, while the less liquid investments were left in the funds, laying the foundations for further problems in the future.

In order to break this negative cycle of endless redemptions the company announced a three-year lock-up that would last till April 2011, when it would deal again with redemptions. The company hoped that the lock-up would give it enough time to sort out the investments in its funds, create liquidity, and that hopefully a wider economic recovery would have taken hold by that time. All this, it was hoped, would alleviate the pressure.

In the meantime the share price in RAB Capital had unsurprisingly fallen such a long way that in the summer of 2010 it was trading at 13p. That was when I started to read up on the company. As so often with value investments, it had appeared on a screen showing companies trading at large discounts to net asset value.

INVESTMENT CASE

There now follows a reasonable amount of information from the company's results to give the reader a better understanding of the issues that were affecting RAB Capital at that time. It looked cheap but could we still hope for a turnaround?

On 28 July 2010, RAB Capital released interim results for the six months ended 30 June 2010. Some important points were as follows:

Overview

- *Encouraging performance across a number of RAB investment strategies.*

- *Assets under management of $1.26bn (December 2009: $1.35bn) after reduction of over $63m from restructured funds.*

- *Continued challenging environment for asset gathering.*

Mid-year financial position

- *Strong balance sheet: net current assets and investments of £93.6m (December 2009: £98.7m).*

- *Net current assets and investments per ordinary share of 19.8p (December 2009: 20.9p).*

- *Interim dividend of 0.10p per ordinary share (June 2009: 0.6p).*

- *Cost base continued to fall.*

First half 2010 trading summary

- *Net income down 13.6% to £8.2m (June 2009: £9.4m).*

- *Loss before tax of £3.3m (June 2009: loss of £2.7m).*

- *Basic and diluted loss per ordinary share of 0.49p (June 2009: loss of 0.43p).*

Important passages from the chairman and chief executive's statement included:

"RAB Capital plc's interim results for the six months to 30 June 2010 reflect the difficult investment environment in the last few months. Although we have made generally good progress against a challenging market in the first quarter, the more volatile environment of May and June made it hard for long/short managers to generate value opportunities. Nonetheless RAB credit, event driven and energy funds all recorded good results as at the end of the half year, RAB Energy in particular delivering over 20% performance in the period and recording positive results even in the most challenging of months. RAB Special Situations continued to improve its liquidity position at the same time as ending the half up approximately 4%."

It was further stated:

"Two specific events after the end of the first half, namely the drop in price of a Special Situations portfolio stock following disappointing oil exploration findings, and the proposed repatriation of Capital by a European bank from RAB fund of funds product have reduced AUM (assets under management). However, the Group continues to see exciting opportunities to bring more strategies and investors to the business and to progress initiatives to improve the efficiency of the platform."

The balance sheet was as follows:

CURRENT ASSETS	£000s
Trade and other receivables	9,935
Current tax assets	3,136
Cash and cash equivalents	39,757
TOTAL CURRENT ASSETS	52,828
LIABILITIES	£000s
TOTAL LIABILITIES	6,905

It had net-net working capital of £45,923,000. With 475,457,670 shares in issue, RAB Capital had a net-net per share of 9.6p. Looking at the non current (i.e. fixed) assets, these came to a total of £56,732,000, which included available-for-sale financial assets of £44,829,000. This represented the group's own investments in their funds.

Adding this figure to the net-net we get a rough net asset value of 19p per share.

The balance sheet seemed to be very liquid, with a high cash position relative to total assets. At that stage in November 2010 the shares were trading at 13p. It seemed that there was still the possibility that management could improve the prospects of the company. It was not without risk, but there was still a business operating here. The big unknown was what the level of redemptions would be once they were allowed again.

What attracted me to the company was the inherent flexibility of its business model. Like nimble service companies, it could fairly painlessly contract its business until profitability was re-established. Once this was achieved, after a certain amount of time a change of name for RAB Capital would help distance it from its past and allow it to grow again. This was actually pretty much management's hope too.

So I bought shares in RAB Capital at 13p in November 2010.

OUTCOME

Unfortunately, time was not on RAB Capital's side. When the Special Situations Fund allowed redemptions to resume again in April 2011, it received requests for *$370m of the $470m fund*.

This was becoming serious, to say the least. It would not immediately hit profitability so much, as no management fees had been charged for the last three years, but the fund had become such a size that its survivability was now in doubt. This certainly did not help sentiment towards RAB Capital.

The resignation of one of the company's more successful fund managers – one on whom the firm had hoped to rebuild their fortunes – proved to be the death knell. This was a major risk inherent in their business model and I'd not paid it enough attention.

Ignoring key personnel risk was my biggest mistake. With this one fund manager leaving, all of a sudden the whole survivability of the company seemed in doubt.

In June 2011 a group of RAB Capital directors offered shareholders 10p per share in cash. It gave us a chance to walk away from this sorry saga. So we took it.

A loss of 3p per share, or 23%.

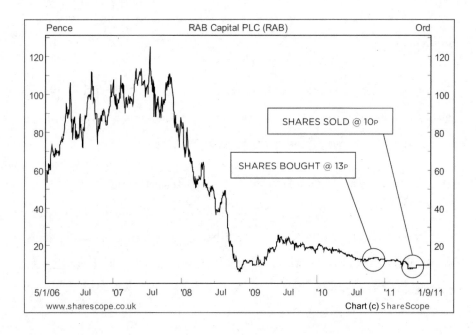

CHAPTER 11. ABBEYCREST

Bought at: 60p (August 2004)

Sold at: 2p (June 2011)

Shares suspended: January 2012

I HAVE EXPERIENCED A FEW investments over the years – and luckily only a few – that looked attractive at the outset but turned into value traps as time passed. One of these was Abbeycrest, the subject of this chapter. Its major problem – also afflicting Alexon Group, another value trap I have tangled with – was an erosion of its working capital, leading to all kinds of trouble.

This is a danger facing all potential value investments. It lurks beneath the comfort of a high net asset value compared to the share price. Marginal profits or losses can seem quite sustainable in the face of this. The hope is simply that better times can be found again. As value investing is mainly a long-only game, a drifting share price is not seen as particularly worrying – the supposed net asset value continues to work as a safety factor. Over time the position shrinks within a portfolio and it seems that the problem is getting smaller. This can actually spell danger.

Companies can be broken in ways that this ignores. Abbeycrest was one of those companies. It had a net asset value materially higher than the current share price, it was still in a position where it could restructure of its own accord, and it had some decent plans for turning things around.

But it failed.

COMPANY BACKGROUND

Abbeycrest was a group engaged in the design, manufacture and distribution of gold and silver jewellery. The group mainly supplied independent jewellery retailers but it also featured in the Argos catalogue. It first listed on the London Stock Exchange in April 1998 in the personal goods sector.

INVESTMENT CASE

When I started looking at the company in May 2004, being concentrated in these marketplaces was not a comfortable place to be. Independent jewellery retailers were in a slowly declining market and the Argos catalogue brought with it the ever-present risk of being dropped from the next edition.

Thankfully, Abbeycrest was working on plenty of initiatives to better secure its future. Production had been moved overseas to lower-cost countries. A new sales office had been opened in the USA. North America was not a great environment for Abbeycrest to operate in (market share was hard to come by), but it was cheap on a balance sheet basis. There was still time to engineer a turnaround for the company.

On 12 May 2004 the company released preliminarily results for the year ended 29 February 2004. These showed that the company was still profitable and paying a dividend. The balance sheet showed a net-net working capital position of £17,848,000. With 24.3m shares outstanding, this gave a net-net per share of 73.5p. Meanwhile the net asset value worked out at 100p. The share price was then at 60p. There was a clear margin of safety based on these numbers. Even if the company operated with a high level of debt (at £20.4m), this had come down between 2003 and 2004 by some £4.6m – an undoubtedly positive sign.

The chairman commented that the year to 29 February 2004 had been one of considerable change and progress in the rebuilding of the group. The group had returned to profit and the reduction in borrowings had accelerated, driven by running the business as efficiently as possible, keeping stocks to a minimum and generating as much cash as possible.

We bought in at 60p in August 2004. The shares traded as high as 79p that year, while the low was 53p.

OUTCOME

Over a year later, on 25 May 2005, the company released results for the year ended 28 February 2005. Group turnover had reduced by 15% to £82.3m, with a basic loss per share of 2.4p. Some important points in the chairman's statement included:

"The current year's sales have been adversely impacted by a legal dispute with a major Chinese supplier, leading to a loss of business.

Our commitment to debt reduction remains and I am pleased that the Group's borrowings continue to reduce despite a year of significant capital expenditure.

"The UK's trading environment has been difficult for Abbeycrest with sales during the key Christmas period generally depressed coupled with a significant reduction in sales levels to one of our major customers.

"Overall, despite a more difficult retail environment in the UK, the Directors are confident of the outlook and prospects of the Group for the year ending 28 February 2006 particularly because of the reduced cost base arising from the relocation of the group's volume manufacturing to Thailand."

Not great, but at least the debt levels had come down – that trend was still in place. The net-net per share still came out at 68p per share from last year's 73p. It was undoubtedly eroding, but a margin of safety was still in place.

However, on 22 August 2005 the company released a rather ominous trading statement:

"At the AGM on 20 July 2005, I highlighted that the jewellery sector was being affected by the slowdown in consumer demand which has been particularly severe in areas of discretionary spending, and which has already led to a cautious approach to stock purchasing by the majority of our customers. To date we have experienced no change to this approach. Indeed, the latest statistics now available which show the volume of jewellery pieces hallmarked across the

UK, compared with last year, <u>worsened considerably in the last month</u>.

"Almost without exception, <u>very recent soundings</u> from key customers and from across the trade in general <u>provide even more cautious indicators for the important pre-Christmas period</u>.

"As a result, we have now decided to <u>downgrade significantly our sales expectations for the year</u>. Consequently, we expect to post a substantial loss for the year ending 28 February 2006.

"Despite the trading difficulties, we are continuing to focus with success on cash management and working capital level reduction across the group. Abbeycrest is confident of its financial position given its strong asset backing … "

On 23 November 2005 the company released interims that showed a loss per share of 15.5p compared to a loss of 7.9p over the same period in the previous year. The working capital position was starting to show the strain on the company. The net-net per share was now 45p (down from 65p) but the NAV still came to 80p per share. The share price was now 22p (down from our 60p purchase). This was getting serious.

The chairman stated:

"As noted in the trading statement issued in August, the <u>jewellery sector has been disproportionally affected</u> by the overall slowdown in the UK economy. Indeed the statistics issued by the assay offices indicate that the level of hallmarking of gold jewellery in the UK is down year-on-year by approximately 25%. The issue of the consumer being reluctant to purchase has been exacerbated by <u>retailers</u>

<u>aggressively de-stocking</u> as their trading performance comes under more pressure. Clearly <u>this has had a fundamental effect</u> on the trading performance of our major UK subsidiary."

At this stage the Abbeycrest share price had fallen to a low for 2005 of 22p. Borrowings had started to rise again and the company found itself in a very uncomfortable position: a sharply weakening balance sheet and an operating environment that was rapidly deteriorating.

In other words, this was a value investment that couldn't hope to bridge the gap between its share price and NAV – or at least, could only do so in one direction.

A value trap had been created. The margin of safety was evaporating. Management initiatives had stemmed the issues for a short period but outside events had overtaken them. The company was no longer in a position to fight these new onslaughts. Liquidity had drained from the company and it now had to consider selling its properties in order to raise much-needed funds. Its capital had been spent and lenders were not willing to put up additional funds.

On 8 May 2006 the company's shares were suspended. This is hardly ever a positive sign. It had been forced on the company: "the group's bankers," said Abbeycrest,

"have asked the Board to <u>arrange alternative facilities </u>for the peak trading period. The directors have therefore sought a refinancing, which is now well advanced, <u>in order to continue normal operations</u>.

"Although not previously envisaged, the refinancing will now include a sale and leaseback of property as the Company is now approaching the build up to its seasonal trading period.

"The directors are confident that the new facilities, including the sale and leaseback of property, will be secured within a matter of days. The directors also remain confident about the future prospects for the Group … "

This was definitely not good news. It meant that the company had difficulty in financing its operations – let alone its rejuvenation. It had now gone from a value stock to something a lot worse.

The next results released on 28 June 2006 showed the damage that it had suffered. Turnover was down by 15%. The business had lost 31.1p per share.

The net-net per share was now 36p compared to last year's 67p. The share price itself sat at 15p. Everything was moving in the wrong direction. It became very difficult to see a way out. The margin of safety kept on eroding, the news flow continued to be very negative with sales continuing to fall, while the price of gold – *the* vital commodity for a jewellery business – continued to rise, putting further pressure on the firm's working capital.

This was a value trap that had taken a few years to develop. The position had seemed quite reasonable at the outset. But by the end it looked dreadful.

With the help of hindsight, was there anything that could have alerted us to the false value offered by the share? Perhaps. It is certainly interesting to note that Abbeycrest started its downward spiral laden with debt, even though the net-net working capital seemed to be strong. The lesson to be learned from this is that high debt levels have to be treated with great caution even if there seems to be a reasonable margin of safety.

If the way for the company to get its performance back to its NAV levels is not reasonably assured, those debt levels can prove deadly. The company's client base was either going through gentle decline (independent retailers) or was a single, and potentially fickle, major retailer (Argos). On top of that the economic downturn meant relentless pressure for ever-lower prices. Against this, a thrifty and creative management team could perhaps have turned things round. But even the greatest management would struggle when faced with surviving such levels of debt at the same time.

The company made no real headway, though debt-reduction at one stage saw some progress. The suspension of the shares in May 2006 was a clear wake-up call. It really was a red flag: the company was at its limit, the banks were starting to feel uncomfortable, and unfortunately they were firmly in the driving seat.

I have not mentioned Abbeycrest's fixed assets yet. When included in the picture, these would have materially raised the net asset value above the net-net working capital position. But the reason I haven't mentioned them is because the company never mentioned them in its reports. It could have been a major fillip if it had been in a position to sell them and ease its financing situation. Unfortunately, what happened only justified my general caution of fixed assets. Nothing could be done with them.

The company struggled on from here for nearly another six years. but the die had been cast and it was now a case to what extent its finance providers would allow it to continue to trade. We sold our position at 2p in June 2011. The sorry tale finally came to a halt in February 2012 when administrators were appointed.

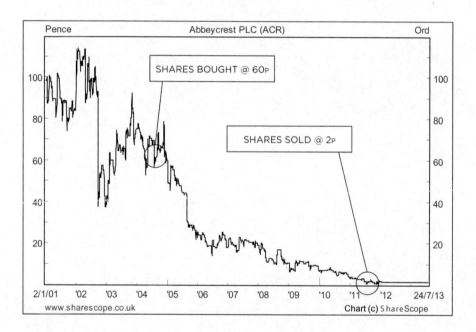

PART IV. DEEP VALUE SHARES OF TOMORROW

CHAPTER 12. BLOOMSBURY PUBLISHING

Bought at: 95p (August 2011)

Still holding at: 127p (June 2013)

THE MARKET'S SHORT-TERMISM and obsession with earnings is a common factor in creating good cheap shares for deep value investors. Even global success stories with fairly strong share prices are not immune to it, as was the case with Bloomsbury Publishing, the British publishing home of *Harry Potter*.

This is a great example of an attractive, cash-rich company which, after analysing, I knew I wanted to invest in – it was just a question of waiting for a general market panic to push short-termist investors into a sell-off.

COMPANY BACKGROUND

Bloomsbury Publishing was founded over 25 years ago, listing on the London Stock Exchange in 1994. The company had grown strongly on the back of the success of the *Harry Potter* novels by J. K. Rowling (the first of which was published in 1997). All seven instalments of this publishing phenomenon had been released when I started looking at the company in 2010 and had sold very well.

Inevitably, however, the stock market had started to fret about life after Potter. Bloomsbury had a lot of cash built up on its balance sheet, but the market was not really focusing on that. Investors were unhappy with the uncertainty and that was not good for sentiment. There was doubt going forward, and the share price reacted by trending downwards. Pre-tax profit had been as high as £17m in 2007 but had fallen to £7.1m in 2009.

On 30 March 2010 the company released preliminary results for the year ended 31 December 2009.

The highlights included:

- revenue of £87.2m (2008 £99.5m)

- basic earnings per share of 6.77p (2008 10.67p)

- net cash of £35m.

The company spoke about the strong line up of its authors besides J. K. Rowling, but there was no denying the fact that the magic of regular *Harry Potter* releases was starting to be missed and this worried the market. It was in no real mood to look at the rest of Bloomsbury Publishing to see if there was anything happening within the group to alleviate the pressure.

Indeed, it seems that even *Harry Potter* was no longer being properly taken into account. After all, Bloomsbury would have the (print) publishing rights to the *Harry Potter* stories for 70 years after the death of its creator. The *Harry Potter* series was still very important to the group and a newly designed edition had been announced along with these results. It would be able to publish it for a long time to come; the story would run for generations.

But the market was concentrating on the here and now. Would cash be squandered on doubtful acquisitions? Would the firm ever again see sales and profits like it had done? In this environment even the *Harry Potter* asset, with all its promise of recurring revenues for perhaps another century, struggled to make itself heard.

INVESTMENT CASE

When we look at Bloomsbury's balance sheet as presented in the preliminary results we see the following ...

CURRENT ASSETS	£00S
Inventories	16,350
Trade and other receivables	47,509
Cash and cash equivalents	35,036
TOTAL CURRENT ASSETS	98,895

Meanwhile total liabilities only came to £26,835,000. This left a net-net working capital position of £72,060,000. With 73,920,795 shares outstanding, Bloomsbury had a net-net working capital position per share of 97p.

The fixed assets amounted to £41m, of which intangibles came to £38m, another instance of an asset-light company – able to weather storms and ready to outperform when the opportunity arises.

Unfortunately, the shares were at this time (summer 2010) trading at 125p – a good premium to the net-net level of 97p.

As I deemed the company's shares to be too expensive for a deep value investment I simply made a note to keep track of Bloomsbury and moved on.

Over time I noticed that the company continued making a number of small acquisitions in different fields of the publishing sector, following on from deals like the purchase of the publishers of *Wisden* in 2008 and *Arden Shakespeare* in January 2009. Many of these boasted recurring revenue characteristics which I thought to be particularly attractive. The *Harry Potter* stories were and are an amazing success for Bloomsbury Publishing, but I knew they were a one-off in their scale. Recycling that cash in recurring revenue generators, though, meant that their contribution could keep on growing indirectly – giving the company a much more stable outlook and eventually, I was sure, leading to a higher rating in the market.

The company was investing the *Potter* windfall in consumer niches where it soon became the biggest publisher. These niches included books on birds, yachting, cricket, writing and cooking. In academic sectors it covered drama, Churchill, religion, philosophy, education, classical culture and fashion. In professional sectors it took on accountancy (PwC, online tax) and law (England & Wales, Scotland, Ireland).

The company was also ably adapting to the revolution of e-publishing. Whilst it did not have the digital rights to *Harry Potter*, this industry sea-change created new opportunities for the company and boasted many attractive features, amongst them:

- much lower return rates from retailers

- much closer relationships with the end user

- faster turnaround between concept and publication

- lower production costs

- reduced cost of failure

- greater visibility of future revenue streams.

So while we waited for the opportunity to buy, the company only grew more attractive.

Our patience finally paid off during a particularly strong sell-off in the stock market in August 2011. We were able to buy the shares at 95p (cf. the net-net level of 97p).

OUTCOME

At the time of writing (June 2013) the shares were trading at 127p, having gone as high as 146p in 2012. This was perhaps not spectacular (though 127p represents an increase of more than 33%), but in the current market environment they are just doing fine.

Though I expect a higher price in future, Bloomsbury was never going to be a share that climbed high quickly – or one that was bought out for a premium by a rival. It is a different kind of value investment to Harvard International, Morson, ArmorGroup et al.

All the while I looked at it, it made profits and paid dividends. It never showed signs of distress. Unlike Bloosmbury, most companies in our portfolio are not well-known names and they are usually loss-making. Dividends tend to be unusual (sometimes you get a capital distribution, a la Gleeson (MJ) Group). It is nice when we are able to own a company that is doing quite well and growing, and which we bought at an objectively good price.

With the success of *Harry Potter*, Bloomsbury has been able to transform its business. It is now much more broadly based, with a far higher proportion of recurring revenues, and is no longer just based in the UK – with offices in the USA, India and Australia. It currently yields over 4.5% and I expect the company to continue growing the business going forward.

The increasing universality of English, coupled with the growth of middle classes in emerging economies, should underpin this, aided by the spread of digital interconnectivity and access to information.

And, of course, another hundred or so years of *Harry Potter* sales.

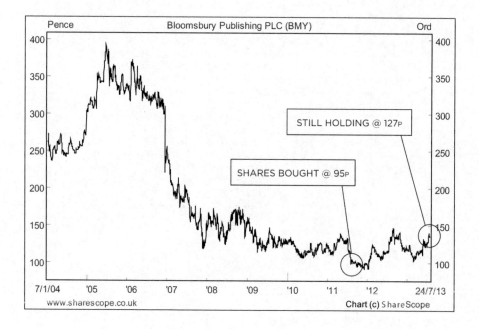

CHAPTER 13. BARRATT DEVELOPMENTS

Bought at: 90p (November 2011)

Still holding at: 330p (June 2013)

S OMETIMES A WHOLE sector can become a value investor's paradise. Virtually every component stock starts showing deep value characteristics. The house-building industry is a good example of this. The industry is *very* cyclical and this creates lots of opportunities for value investors. However, when the sector is in crisis, risk is also at its highest – and it is still very possible to get caught out. One needs to be cautious, even when a share seems to be the bargain of the century.

Our investment in Barratt Developments took a long time in coming as we wanted to be certain of the company's value before committing ourselves.

COMPANY BACKGROUND

A snapshot of the share price of Barratt Developments is actually a perfect illustration of the volatility in this sector. The shares reached a high of 845p in 2007. In 2008 they reached a low of *25.3p*. These dramatic price movements came as a result of the industry being engulfed by the recession that started in 2007. Many house-builders were hit hard. The speed of the downturn caught lots of people out.

A quirk of how house-builders are structured makes them vulnerable in downturns. The current asset side of their balance sheets shows their main asset of inventories (i.e. the land bank), while their main liability tends to be the loans and borrowings (either long or short-term financed) used to buy this land bank.

In 'normal' times this is not really a strange situation to be in. It's how the industry operates. However, what happened from 2007 onwards was the dangerous situation of these land bank valuations having to be impaired (i.e. written down) while the amount of debt on the liabilities side stayed the same or grew.

As a result, balance sheets came under great pressure. Many house-builders had to seek further financing, either through rights issues, increased bank loans (or a combination of the two) or partial sales etc. This was an industry-wide event and few could avoid the carnage that was meted out. Media reports made it seem as if house-building in the UK was finished.

This happened in other countries, too. Ireland, Spain and the USA all had severe downturns in their house-building sectors.

NON-INVESTMENT CASE

The results Barratt Developments released on 10 September 2008 for the financial year ended 30 June 2008 give us an idea about the state of play at that time. Important points included:

- profit before tax of £137.3m (2007 £424m)

- basic earnings per share of 25p (2007 115p)

- exceptional cost totalling £255m and comprising £208.4m impairment of inventories, £30.7m impairment of goodwill and intangible assets.

The chief executive's statement, under the heading 'Current trading and outlook', didn't contain anything to get too excited about – it was all pretty cautious.

The group finance director's review was cautious, too:

> "This has been a very challenging financial year for all house-builders. We have taken appropriate measures to reflect the significant market downturn. Earnings have proved robust and we have maintained asset quality. The refinancing and revised covenant package recently put in place was an important step in ensuring that the group has strong foundations to weather market conditions which are likely to remain difficult for the foreseeable future."

The balance sheet as presented in these results looked like this as at 30 June 2008:

CURRENT ASSETS	£M	£M
	2008	2007
Inventories	4,830	4,739.9
Trade and other receivables	100.9	141.7
Cash and cash equivalents	32.8	182.1
Current tax assets	20.6	0
TOTAL CURRENT ASSETS	4,984.3	5,063.7

LIABILITIES	£M	£M
CURRENT LIABILITIES	2008	2007
Loans and borrowings	(653.7)	(26.7)
Trade and other payables	(1,163.8)	(1,484.4)
Current tax liabilities	0	(58.2)
NON-CURRENT LIABILITIES		
Loans and borrowings	(1,031.5)	(1,456.6)
Trade and other payables	(242.1)	(100.6)
Retirement benefit obligations	(70.1)	(78.3)
Deferred tax liabilities	(22.7)	0
Deferred financial instrument – swaps	(9.5)	0
TOTAL LIABILITIES	(3,194.0)	(3,204.8)

It is interesting to observe that, although the overall total liabilities were pretty similar to the 2007 level, there was a lot of movement in the current and non-current liabilities. Under current liabilities the loans and borrowings had shot up in 2008. The non-current liabilities (i.e. those longer than a year), loans and borrowings, had come down somewhat, but this really meant that the company had less long-term financing in place and was becoming more reliant on short-term finance. Not really a happy position to be in should the market contract further going forward.

The net-net working capital position worked out at £1,7903m (2007: £1,858.9m).

The number of shares was 346.7m (2007: 262.8m), so the net-net worked out at 516p per share – a surprisingly high level compared to a share price that in 2008 only traded as high as 310p and as low as 25p. This looked like the bargain of the century. There was a huge margin of safety.

But it wasn't quite so simple.

Looking at the current assets we could see that these were mainly made up of inventories – i.e. the land bank – which could still prove to be very vulnerable to writedowns. Though the company had impaired these by £208m, compared to the level of inventories of £4,830m this seemed to be a very modest impairment – just 4.3%. After all, the state of the market indicated that the outlook was pretty severe (something management reiterated in these results).

So, although the net-net looked very high in comparison to the share price, there seemed to be considerable risk on the downside going forward.

Too much risk, in fact.

THE WAITING GAME

Once these downward trends get established it takes a certain amount of time for the negative forces to play out. The house-building sector could become interesting but at that point in time we thought it was better to stay on the sidelines.

It was now important to keep an eye on the house-builders and read their statements carefully. They all had to report more or less on the same trends affecting the industry. If one of them had to writedown the value of their land bank then all the others would almost certainly face the same pressures (allowing for differences between regions and so on).

It was simply a matter of waiting for the real industry pain to manifest itself and see which company would be the first to announce big write-offs and seek rescue financing.

And in June 2008, Taylor Wimpey announced the writedown of the value of their land bank and building sites by £660m, confirming it would be looking to raise cash from shareholders. McCarthy & Stone, another house-builder, was reported to be working with its bankers to restructure some £800m of its debt. During that summer, the news flow from the UK housing sector continued to highlight the difficulties facing the industry. In June it was reported that the number of new houses built in Britain had fallen by nearly 60% from the previous year. The share prices of all house-builders had fallen substantially from their previous peaks – plenty of potential value was being created for investors.

The rest of 2008 brought little happiness to the industry, but from 2009 it seemed that things were starting to pick up. Some stability was returning and the survival of the industry was no longer really questioned.

We now move forward to 23 September 2009, when Barratt Developments announced a rights issue, raising £720m. During that month several other house-builders did so as well, including Redrow (£156m), Galliford Try (£125m) and Bovis Homes (£60m). Bellway had raised £44m that August.

Raising £720m meant a relatively big issue for Barratt Developments (618.4m new shares) – it obviously needed a lot of money in order to recapitalise and to be able to start buying land again. Happily, the land that would now be bought was priced at substantially lower prices compared to the previous peak and this would enable Barratt Developments to improve its margins.

The board also announced certain amendments to its existing financing arrangements, conditional on the completion of the placing and the rights issue. The banks would provide part of the finance but further finance would be raised from the shareholders of Barratt Developments. This was an important development. The company had now been recapitalised. It could endure further stress in the market and was stabilised for the foreseeable future.

Now it was time to start looking for positive signs. Did builders no longer need to writedown land bank valuations? Even better, could we see that some of them were starting to buy land again? This was crucial. It would signal that land prices had stabilised and that balance sheet valuations of house-builder land banks were close to reality. The risk of further big writedowns would have fallen substantially and a reliable net-net could be found.

INVESTMENT CASE

It wasn't until November 2011 that such positive signs seemed to appear and we started looking seriously at Barratt again.

Its shares were trading at 90p, having been lower in the meantime. We had recently sold some shares in Bovis Homes. These had looked cheap compared to balance sheet valuations and subsequently benefitted from early confidence returning to the sector. That confidence was mostly built on the fact that, with many of the house-builders having raised additional capital, the immediate danger of industry insolvencies seemed now to have past. This certainly was good news: although the industry still suffered from a lack of mortgage availability, firms were now in a much stronger position to deal with difficulties.

Barratt's shares seemed to have moved quite a bit on the back of this improved sentiment. And on 14 September 2011 the company released annual results for the year ended 30 June 2011. All the highlights pointed to a more positive operating environment in line with its competitors.

Turning to the balance sheet we could see:

CURRENT ASSETS	£M
Inventories	3,296.8
Trade and other receivables	58.7
Cash and cash equivalents	72.7
Current tax assets	3.2
TOTAL CURRENT ASSETS	3,431.4

LIABILITIES	£M
NON-CURRENT LIABILITIES	
Loans and borrowings	(405.5)
Trade and other payables	(352.5)
Retirement benefit obligations	(11.8)
Derivative financial instruments – swaps	(37.0)
TOTAL NON-CURRENT LIABILITIES	(806.8)
CURRENT LIABILITIES	
Loans and borrowings	(11.2)
Trade and other payables	(1,027.2)
TOTAL LIABILITIES	(1,845.2)

The net-net working capital position worked out at £1,586.2m. With 961.4m shares outstanding, we were now looking at a net-net working capital position of 164p per share. (Remember that the shares were then trading at 90p.)

It was interesting to see how the balance sheet had been transformed since 30 June 2008. Then total borrowings had been £1,685m. Now they were down to £416.5m. The company was clearly in better shape after the 2009 fundraising.

The chairman's statement under the heading 'New land to improve margins' further stated:

> "Since we re-entered the land market in mid-2009 we have had two good years of land buying and invested a total of £981.3m. We have secured terms on around 22,000 plots and this will represent the foundation of our future business and margin growth … "

This all sounded quite positive and was in line with what others had said. Most house-builders had returned to buying land again. The lower cost of the recently bought land helped margins and profitability to grow.

There were a few factors at work that made the British housing market quite attractive in comparison to many other markets – for example, Ireland (oversupply), Spain (oversupply) and the USA (mortgage foreclosures).

Even at the depth of the recent recession the industry knew that Britain still had a severe housing shortage. Prior to the downturn, the housing stock had been growing by 185,000 units a year against government forecasts of an annually required 240,000 by 2016 in order to meet the demand of the growing population. Only 80,000 new house-building starts were forecast for the 2008/9 financial year.

This made for a strong market outlook. In the UK the main obstacle to any recovery in the house-building industry was the lack of available mortgage finance and not a severe overhang of new houses that still needed to be sold.

So we bought into Barratt Developments at 90p in November 2011.

OUTCOME

By November 2012 we seemed to be at the beginning of a cyclical recovery in profitability for house-builders and the trend looked set to continue for some years. At the time of writing, many of the house-builders' shares were trading at near or slight premiums to their net asset valuations. The market was now focusing on earnings again. A need for healthy balance sheets had been replaced by the usual focus on income statements and this should continue pushing prices until we hit the next cyclical high again.

Going forward we can expect some house-builders to be able to revalue their land banks at higher levels. This will have a very positive impact on their balance sheets. It will be a while before we are full circle again and it is time to think about selling.

At the time of writing, Barratt Developments shares were trading at 330p, an increase of 267%.

Pence   Barratt Developments PLC (BDEV)   Ord

STILL HOLDING @ 330P

SHARES BOUGHT @ 90P

www.sharescope.co.uk   Chart (c) ShareScope

CHAPTER 14. MJ GLEESON

Bought at: 101p (average price, most shares bought during 2009)

Still holding at: 337p (June 2013)

COMPANY BACKGROUND

MJ GLEESON HAS BEEN LISTED on the London Stock Exchange since 1960 and is now over a hundred years old. The company is part of the construction and materials sector.

It has two main divisions: house-building in the north of England, and a strategic land division mainly focusing on the south of England. This second part of the company makes MJ Gleeson a rather unique company that does not lend itself to easy comparison with others in its sector. Its strategic land division was also the main reason for our investment.

A more diversified company than Barratt Developments, over the years 2008–11 Gleeson was still exposed to the same forces affecting Barratt and other house-builders. Gleeson dealt with these in a different way. Rather uniquely, the company had also continued to be debt-free – which put it in a much stronger position when confronting asset impairments and write-offs.

I first took a look at Gleeson in the summer of 2008, when the whole construction sector came under great pressure and share prices in general were falling (a process described in Chapter 13 on Barratt Developments). Gleeson had started 2008 at over 300p. During that year it touched a low of 57p.

INVESTMENT CASE

The results released by the company on 25 February 2009 played an important role in prompting my investment. The balance sheet as at 31 December 2008 showed:

CURRENT ASSETS	£000s
Inventories	77,359
Trade and other receivables	61,838
UK corporation tax	1,893
Cash and cash equivalents	7,078
TOTAL CURRENT ASSETS	148,168

LIABILITIES	£000s
CURRENT LIABILITIES	
Trade and other payables	(42,390)
Provisions	(2,401)
NON-CURRENT LIABILITIES	
Provisions	(4,400)
Deferred tax liabilities	(328)
TOTAL LIABILITIES	(49,519)

The net-net working capital position was £98,649,000 and the number of shares in issue at the time was 52,334,000, resulting in a net-net working capital position per share of 188p (versus a share price of 109p at the time).

It is interesting how this balance sheet was structured compared to Barratt Developments. Gleeson had no debt; Barratt, heading into the recession, £1,685m. Although both companies still had to face the worst of the recession at the time we started looking at them, the absence of debt in Gleeson's case took some of the pressure off its balance sheet.

As discussed with Barratt, house-builders suffer in downturns from writedowns on their assets but debt levels that remain static at the same time. At least one of those deadly factors didn't exist here. Gleeson would have to impair its land bank more or less to the same extent as every house-builder had to. But even if Gleeson had to *halve* the value of its inventories (an apocalyptic worst-case scenario), the net-net working capital position would still have been £59,915,500 or 114p per share (cf. share price of 109p).

For Barratt, on the other hand, it would have been disastrous. Based on its figures in Chapter 13, writing down its inventories by 50% would have driven working capital into the negative by *£2.5bn*. The company would have been in very big trouble.

At the time we had no idea how bad the recession would be, but I knew which company I preferred. Gleeson offered a much greater margin of safety than Barratt Developments ever could. Looking more closely at its structure, we could also see that the business in the south concentrated on buying land to be sold to other house-builders once planning permission had been received. The British housing market that seemed best able to survive the Great Recession was that of London and the southeast – leaving the firm particularly well-positioned for when the slump eventually passed.

We therefore started accumulating shares in the business at 109p, acquiring most of our holding over 2009 at an average price of 101p.

OUTCOME

On 24 September 2009 the group announced preliminary figures which showed "downward asset revaluations of £44.6m, a pre-tax loss but also that cash balances had now risen to £16m". The net-net after these results still worked out at £81.3m or 155p per share.

The industry and economic trend was downwards but we still had a margin of safety with the price we had paid. Even though this statement dealt with the past, Gleeson mentioned that since the year-end it had seen some signs of improvement in buyer interest.

We had to wait for better news. When the interim announcement was made on 24 February 2010, the highlights were a definite improvement of the previous releases. Under key financial points the company announced:

- revenue from continuing operations increased by 17%

- pre-tax profits on continuing operations of £0.3m (2008: loss of 23.7m)

- net cash in the period increased by £9.5m to £20.4m

- concluding that the group had excess cash, the board decided to pay a special dividend per share of 15p.

This was much more like it. The net-net working capital position was now £77.3m or 147p per share. It seemed that the worst was over.

Profitability was marginal at this stage, but a further period of asset writedowns seemed to be over for the group and confidence was returning. The payment of a special dividend was certainly very welcome news and a sign that the company's management had confidence in the immediate outlook.

It is a rare event indeed for an investment to pay a special dividend like this. It often seems to be a good idea to return excess cash to shareholders – it is theirs in the first place, after all – but cash is usually squandered on bad acquisition or inappropriate share buybacks. Value investors like share buybacks, but only when they are done at a discount to NAV, thereby increasing their investment's NAV per share. Unhappily, most share buybacks are done at a *premium* to NAV and are rather designed to increase the earnings per share while little regard is given to the NAV of the underlying securities. Management often likes this, as it helps them to reach earnings per share targets, as well as making the management share option scheme perform so much better.

As the recession took hold, management also took corrective action by selling and closing divisions as necessary. A social housing maintenance business (part of its northern house-building side) was sold (at a profit) and Gleeson Commercial Property development disposed of its remaining commercial property sites. Meanwhile, the southern land division was retained.

At the time of writing (June 2013), Gleeson shares were trading at 337p (an increase of 234%). This was still at a discount to NAV and showed that the share price has so far not reacted as strongly as some of the other house-builders. That may still come – or we may see some consolidation in the industry, and the emergence of one or two interested suitors. Several house-builders have commented on the fact that they are "light" on building plots in the south of England, right where Gleeson's strategic land division has its holdings.

As we watch and wait, we are fairly relaxed. There is only one aspect of the investment we will be monitoring particularly closely. Under 'Tax', the company has announced "£89m of tax losses which can be carried forward indefinitely". This tax loss is quite big in relation to the capitalisation of Gleeson and will bear watching. It is actually potentially a big positive as the tax position should be helped by these provisions, they are so big when taking the total value of the company into consideration.

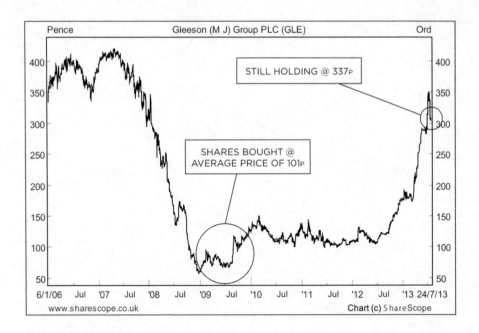

STILL HOLDING @ 337P

SHARES BOUGHT @
AVERAGE PRICE OF 101P

Pence   Gleeson (M J) Group PLC (GLE)   Ord

400

350

300

250

200

150

100

50

6/1/06 Jul '07 Jul '08 Jul '09 Jul '10 Jul '11 Jul '12 Jul '13 24/7/13

www.sharescope.co.uk   Chart (c) ShareScope

CHAPTER 15. FRENCH CONNECTION

Bought at: 29p (December 2009)

Some sold at: 112p (February 2011)

Rest held at: 29p (June 2013)

COMPANY BACKGROUND

W HEN I STARTED LOOKING at clothing retailer French Connection in early 2009, it was looking rather tired. For years the company had relied on a very successful marketing campaign based around its notorious 'FCUK' branding. On the back of this campaign, French Connection had become one of the better-known brands in the UK and overseas. The company had a presence in many countries in Europe, North America and the Far East.

But things were looking less promising now.

In 2006 its shares had traded as high as 280p, when profits peaked at £12.6m. Since then they had been on a slide. In 2009 the share price reached a high of 73p. Later it would reach a low of 28p.

INVESTMENT CASE

We had spotted the shares early in 2009 as they slid precipitously into value territory. We ignored them for the time being. When, in October 2009, they fell to new lows, I decided to have another look. The firm had last reported on 17 September 2009, with a half-year statement for the first six months ended 31 July 2009.

Some of the highlights included:

- turnover increased by 4% to £116.9m (2008: £112.4m) with the consolidation of its Japan business and new UK/Europe sites offset by declines in wholesale turnover

- like-for-like sales in UK/Europe had grown by 2%, driven by a resilient performance from ladies wear and e-commerce

- gross margin was 50.8% compared to 51.8% previously, primarily affected by weakness of sterling

- underlying savings of 9% had been achieved in the controllable cost base

- the group loss before taxation was £12.8m (compared to £5.4m in 2008, excluding £1.9m gain on the disposal of leased property)

- the balance sheet remained strong with no borrowings, closing net cash of £23.7m and tightly controlled inventory.

The chairman commented on the results:

"Following on from the second half of last year, our business continues to be severely affected by difficult retail environments in all of our markets around the world. In addition to the underlying trading issues we have faced over recent periods, this has had a severe impact on our financial performance during the first six months of the year. Both turnover and gross margin have been weak and although we have made substantial savings in operating expenses, the trading result has declined significantly compared with last year. The core business continues to show encouraging development with continuing growth in French Connections ladies wear.

"In the light of the trading conditions experienced over the past year the Board has been engaged in a strategic review of all of our businesses with a view to enhancing both profitability and cash generation. The review is focused on the international activities of the group, loss-making business segments and central overheads. Initial results from the review have included the closure of our Northern European retail operations and a reduction in head office staffing. It is our intention to implement further measures over the next six months.

"Looking to the second half of the financial year we are aiming to achieve a small improvement on the last operating result from our current operations while also making strategic changes necessary to stem the recent losses."

Not a lot to get excited about, but at least the board was aware of the issues and seemed to be tackling them proficiently.

The balance sheet in the results of 17 September 2009 looked like this:

ASSETS	£M
NON-CURRENT ASSETS	
Intangible assets	2.4
Property, plant and equipment	14.1
Investments in joint ventures	2.1
Deferred tax assets	5.2
CURRENT ASSETS	
Inventories	54.8
Trade and other receivables	32.1
Current tax receivables	0.2
Cash and cash equivalents	23.7
TOTAL ASSETS	134.6

LIABILITIES	£M
NON-CURRENT LIABILITIES	
Finance leases	(0.3)
Deferred tax liabilities	(0.8)
CURRENT LIABILITIES	
Trade and other payables	(48.1)
Current tax payable	(0.1)
Derivative financial instruments	(0.9)
TOTAL LIABILITIES	(50.2)

The net-net working capital position was £60.6m, with 96m shares outstanding, giving a net-net per share of 63.1p – a *substantial* margin of safety compared to a share price of 29p. Including the fixed assets (or non-current assets) of £23.8m – but not the intangibles – gave a net asset value per share of 87p. This looked like a great buy.

But there were a couple of extra things to bear in mind before we bought.

With retailers it is always very important to understand that their retail property portfolio will carry substantial leasehold commitments that in general run for several years going forward. In this case, French Connection tended to occupy the best sites available. This was actually reassuring: it meant that the group could conceivably re-assign these leases if the need arose.

The other risk inherent to fashion retailers is that the current asset item of inventories may only be worth a fraction of the value which appears on the balance sheet. With short cycles in fashion, management getting a trend wrong can have significant consequences on top-line sales and in the carried values of inventories.

Fortunately this did not appear to be the case with French Connection at that moment in time either. Even if we wrote down the value of the inventories by 50% (assuming a disastrous sequence of fashion blunders) the net-net per share was still at 34.5p. Not as good as 63.1p – but still above the share price.

So in October 2009 we bought shares in the company at 29p.

OUTCOME

On 15 March 2010 the company released preliminary results for the year ended 31 January 2010. Under the heading 'Restructuring to return French Connection to Profitability' some important points included:

- the sale of Nicole Farhi (a standalone division of French Connection) to OpenGate Capital for a consideration of up to £5m

- closure of the majority of the under-performing French Connection retail stores in the US and projected exit of the Japanese market

- reported group loss after tax of £24.9m (2009: £16.4m)

- strong balance sheet with closing net cash of £35.7m and proposed dividend of 0.5p for the year (2009: total dividend of 1.7p).

So, not the most exciting news yet. But at least the cash position remained strong, the net-net was still £52.1m (or 54.3p per share), and NAV stood at 72.8p. These results were certainly not helpful, but the balance sheet could take the strain and we still had a margin of safety. The price now stood at 48p.

The company's next results announcement was the half-year statement for the six months ended 31 July 2010. Highlights included:

- substantial improvement in operating result

- positive impact from restructuring, which was largely complete

- turnover up 4%, gross margin up 2.4%, profit before tax of £0.2m (2009: -£7.7m)

- cash balance of £30.2m – well ahead of last year by £6.5m.

The chairman commented: "I am pleased with the substantial improvement in operating results and confident that French Connection is back on track … "

He was not the only one. The share price started to respond to this more positive news. It hit 50p at the time. In December 2011, it traded at 70p. It seemed that French Connection was now seen as a recovery play. Having traded as high as 280p in 2006 there was still a long way to go if recovery really took hold.

The next results were released on 19 September 2011. These were the half-year results for the six months ended 31 July 2011. Highlights included:

- revenue up 7%

- profit before tax of £30.7m (2010: £0.2m)

- closing net cash of $30.9m (2010: 30.2m)

- interim dividend increased 20% to 0.6p.

Some key chairman comments included:

"I am happy to report that, in tough retail trading conditions, <u>we achieved growth in like-for-like retail sales and a substantial increase in both wholesale and licensing income</u>. We are reporting a profit after tax in the first half of the financial year for the first time since 2008 and we are firmly back on a growth path."

He also stated:

> "The balance sheet remains <u>very strong, with £33.9m of cash and no debt</u>. The 20% increase in interim dividend reflects the group's profitability and cash generation and the board's confidence in the future … "

The shares continued to rise on the back of these positive comments. We sold part of our position in February 2011 at 112p (a nice profit of 315%). The price reached a high of 134p that year but then started to fall off again, as worries about the general outlook for the retail sector and French Connection's position within it started to resurface.

A WORK IN PROGRESS

At the time of writing (June 2013), the stock was back at 27p. Yes, it travelled all the way back down. While the firm recovering its operating performance did get it back to profitability, it struggled to grow that profitability from a still low base while the UK continued in a recessionary slump.

There are some reasonably obvious ways forward, and good reason to keep holding its shares (we bought ours back as the price fell again).

The initial restructuring that has been implemented focused on the firm's international operations, shrinking these till the company was left with just the profitable parts. A new, more deep-rooted restructuring seems to be possible – and called for. With e-commerce becoming ever more important, underperforming stores need to be repositioned or closed, and warehouse efficiencies must be tackled. This will take longer to accomplish, and longer still for the effects to be felt on the balance sheet. But it is a definite way forward.

Price points are also a place where the firm has room for improvement. Interestingly, the management of Moss Bros tell me they have no problem selling plenty of French Connection suits in their stores. The brand is still very strong. In their opinion, French Connection's problem is simply that its retail stores are perceived as too expensive compared to its competitors.

The company released an interim management statement on 21 November 2012, which finished:

> " ... we remain confident that the initiatives being implemented and tight cost management will result in a steady and significant improvement in the revenue and gross margins in the business and will therefore have a positive impact on group profitability across the next two financial years ... "

The British retail sector continues to be very tough, but French Connection continues to operate with a strong balance sheet, giving us a margin of safety. On 13 March 2013 French Connection released preliminary results for the year ended 31 January 2013. Important details included:

- revenue down 8% to £197.3 million (2012: £215.4 million).

- underlying loss before tax of £7.2 million (2012: profit of £4.6 million)

- closing net cash of £28.5m (2012: £34.2 million) and no debt.

So the cash on the balance sheet is still slightly higher than the firm's market capitalisation (£28.5m versus £26.88m).

The firm has also seen strong progress in implementing improvement initiatives, even if the trend is still negative: the net-net is now 52p per share, as opposed to 60p on the same date in 2012 (and 63p at the time of our original investment). So we have lost part of our margin of safety at this stage, but not too much – and the chairman's words in the results are promisingly bullish about an imminent return to profitability. We will have to keep a close eye on future releases from the company, but at this stage it still looks attractive at the current valuations.

CHAPTER 16. NORCON

Bought at: 23.5p (average price, bought between March 2012 and April 2013)

Still hold at: 13p (June 2013)

COMPANY BACKGROUND

N ORCON IS THE HOLDING company for Norconsult Telematics Limited, an international project management and outsourcing services business which has its head office in Cyprus and operates principally in the telecommunications sector. Norcon – incorporated in the Isle of Man – has only been listed since July 2008 on the London Stock Exchange's AIM market. It was placed at 69p.

Norconsult has provided project management services in more than 20 countries around the world since 1957. Its projects range from simple studies of limited scope and duration, to a US$233m contract over several years under which Norconsult was responsible for managing a $5bn infrastructure investment.

It describes it business and market advantage as follows:

"The technical complexities of fixed line and mobile telephone systems, together with the associated data networks, have increased dramatically since Norconsult was formed. Operators, particularly in emerging countries, regularly use external consults to assist them install, upgrade and operate their various telephone networks. With approximately 3,000 suitably qualified consultants to draw from, Norconsult regards itself as the market leader in its core markets.

"Barriers to entry are high and include access to appropriate qualified and experienced consultants, financial stability and past references from customers."

INVESTMENT CASE

I first came across Norcon during a screening process, looking for stocks trading at substantial discounts to their net asset value. The most recent statement I could find was the one released on 13 April 2012 for the 12 months ended 31 December 2011. Highlights included:

- revenue of $66.6m (2010: $68.6m)

- profit before tax of $6.2m

- cash at year-end increased to $12.5m (2010: $12.1m)

- client engagements in core markets renewed, in addition to new mandates secured in key expansion territories.

The chairman commented:

"I am pleased that Norcon has managed to deliver another good year, in spite of global economic pressures. Thanks to our long-term relations with key customers and great work by our team we remain resilient. We have made investments into our future as the company continues to increase its geographical reach, as well as the services we offer to our clients. I firmly believe that our core strengths support our long-term growth prospects."

The balance sheet at 31 December 2011 looked like this:

ASSETS	US$
NON-CURRENT ASSETS	
Property, plant equipment	159,957
Investments in associated undertakings	590,211
CURRENT ASSETS	
Trade and other receivables	35,263,743
Cash at bank and in hand	12,456,037
TOTAL ASSETS	48,469,948

LIABILITIES	US$
NON-CURRENT LIABILITIES	
Employees terminal benefits	10,514,890
CURRENT LIABILITIES	
Trade and other payables	6,542,573
Borrowings	5,327,290
Current tax liabilities	733,044
TOTAL LIABILITIES	23,117,797

The net-net working capital came to $24,601,983 and 48,800,808 shares outstanding. The US$ to £GBP exchange rate was 1.58 at that time. The net-net per share was therefore 32p.

As can be seen, the company had very little in fixed assets, so the net asset value was virtually the same as the net-net working capital level. It was trading at 20p in November 2012. Even though it had been consistently profitable the share price had never really reflected this (its high was 89p in 2009).

Looking at the results, it was not immediately obvious why this stock should be trading at a net-net working capital level. It made profits, paid a dividend that yielded 5%, had a lot of cash and the latest statement was pretty positive. This is not the usual background of a net-net stock.

Were there any downsides?

As the company has been in existence since the 1950s it did have a relatively large pension obligation liability of some $10.5m. It is always a good idea with longer-established companies to check the pension liability situation. It can be substantial. Sometimes firms can start to look like a pension fund with an operating company attached to them.

And pension fund trustees have a lot of power. Most pertinently to investors in value stocks, if a company enters liquidation such trustees *have priority claims on any surplus assets.* In other words, they must be paid before shareholders receive any payouts. So it is always a good idea to read the total statement and look for any comments concerning the pension fund position. It can mean the difference between a comfortable margin of safety – and no margin at all.

Fortunately, in this case, although compared to the total assets of the company it was a meaningful figure, the overall liabilities came to less than half of the current assets in the business.

It seemed that the reasons for its price weakness lay elsewhere. The shareholder list of Norcon was pretty weak, with only one major British shareholder on it. That neglect can become self-fulfilling. With a market capitalisation of less than £10m, it seemed to have simply fallen off the radar of potential investors. This wasn't entirely reassuring. As a value investor, I do like to see at least a few institutions on the shareholder list – for comfort, if nothing else.

Nevertheless, Norconsult had been consistently profitable since 1997 and in the period from 1997 to 2007 Norcon had declared dividends of, on aggregate, $30.5m. Norconsult's business had grown steadily in recent years and the directors believed this growth was set to continue. The company was a leader in its field and punched well above its weight against some pretty big competitors, none of whom had as good a rival track record.

In a growing marketplace, it was not too optimistic to expect such a high-performing minnow to be bought by a much bigger competitor who wanted to acquire a seat at the top table in one move. And I like companies with Norcon's type of business model: the firm is a service provider on long-term contracts in an increasingly complicated marketplace which continued to provide new growth opportunities. The company could also explore other regions in the world where it was currently not active (something that was under consideration).

It was not without its vulnerabilities. In the past the company had been very reliant on one customer in the Middle East, a relationship that had existed for many years. However, Norcon was now so embedded in the client's organisation that it would take some considerable time to unwind the relationship. And it was something that management was very aware of. A lot of its time was focused on reducing this over-reliance. As recently as 24 September 2012 the company announced it had secured a large new project in Indonesia, with Indosat, which was expected to run for a number of years.

So we bought shares at 29p in May 2012, when they were trading at a discount to the net-net position of 31p, building a 3% stake in the company.

OUTCOME

On 20 September 2012 Norcon released results for the six-month period ended 30 June 2012. Financial headlines included:

- revenue of $25.3m (2011: $35.9m)

- loss after tax of $0.5m (2011: $2.4m profit)

- negative net cash balance of $1.5m (2011: $1.1m)

- significant proportion of outstanding balances collected post period end

- net cash improved by $7.5m since period end

- pro forma loss per share of $0.01 (2011: $0.05).

Operational headlines included an admission that "delays in the commencement of certain projects have held back revenue and profit growth, albeit the turnover for the first half is broadly in line with expectations: slower than anticipated ramp of 4G projects in key

Middle East marketplace, but with multi-year contracts now in place. Some delay in the roll-out of other international projects that are now being worked through and supported by new hires."

The firm also said that "geographical and service line growth have remained key priorities", including:

- new client engagements secured in Southeast Asia

- first two telecom client engagements secured in USA

- pipeline in Middle East, Africa and Europe continued to strengthen

- strong client retention record maintained

- developments in the telecom industry continued to support demand for Norcon's specialised telecom services.

The chairman commented:

"This first half performance reflects a combination of factors which have served to significantly impact our profitability in the short term. We continue to believe strongly in our opportunity to secure profitable and sustainable growth by expanding into growth markets and new services. We have pushed ahead with our investments in that opportunity, expanding our presence into the US and continuing to win important mandates in Southeast Asia.

"Those investments, however, have come alongside delays to certain new projects, thereby reducing our margins. We are taking important steps to improve our performance in our core market in the Middle East, while at the same time, continue to expect that the <u>investments made in expansion will deliver returns from 2013 onwards</u>."

Not really disastrous – but unforeseen delays are never helpful. We were happy to hold onto the shares; we expected the firm to return to growth at some stage in the future. With its long track record – the longest in this particular industry – operating in international markets that continue to grow, with new technologies on their way, it seemed that the ingredients were in place for a better share price performance at some stage.

On 23 April 2013 the company released final results for the 12 months ended 31 December 2012. This showed a decline in revenue and a slight drop in the net-net position. Meanwhile the price stood at a very low 14p – a big drop from 29p. This seemed to indicate the company was in all kinds of trouble.

And yet the company remained profitable, and had a long history of being so. To my mind, the only mistake was buying in too quickly, so I have added to my position, bringing my average purchase price down.

Given the company's head office in Cyprus, you don't have to look too far for the cause of its unhappy performance. Cyprus's financial woes in 2013, and the widely reported difficulties with the movement of funds from that country, can have only made things difficult for Norcon.

But they don't seem to have had any serious impact on the firm. In the long term, I still think the company remains an interesting value proposition. The balance sheet is in good shape, it has the longest track record in the industry, contracts tend to be multi-year and the market in which it operates is growing.

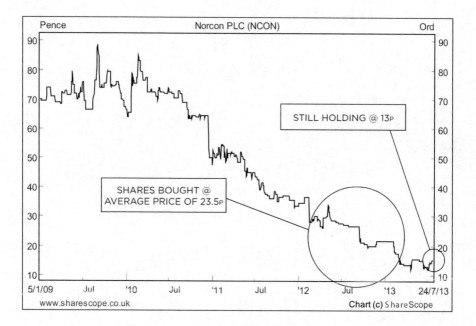

CHAPTER 17. RECORD

Bought at: 9.75p (March 2012)

Still hold at: 34p (June 2013)

F INDING THE PERFECT value stock is a rare experience. In many ways 'perfect' and 'value' are a bit of a contradiction: most value stocks come with a lot of negative baggage (hence the value). But Record came very close to being the perfect value stock. To find a share trading at working capital levels, profitable and debt-free, is unusual. When such a net-net is in the service sector, it's even rarer, since they only appear when the sector or company outlook is particularly negative.

As mentioned in Part I, these service companies are in my experience the most attractive stocks to invest in. They tend to be fairly asset light (with, in more normal times, a high ROCE ratio[1]), and when they do turn around their share price performance can be quite spectacular. They are as good as any high-growth company – with a much lower risk profile.

---

1   This is a measure of the return generated on the invested capital – the higher the ratio, the more attractive the investment case.

COMPANY BACKGROUND

In March 2012, while looking for stocks that had hit new 52-week lows, I came across Record, a specialist currency manager for institutional clients.

I had never heard of the company before. A quick glance at its last results showed that it had been a very profitable business with a strong balance sheet. The company had been set up by Mr Neil Record, who had for many years been involved in the foreign currency markets, and was first listed on the London Stock Exchange in December 2007.

Record's customers tended to be institutional clients like pension funds and mutual funds who needed to hedge their foreign currency exposures as a result of investing in international capital markets. Since the 1980s these types of institutions have greatly increased their holdings of foreign assets and this development played into the hands of firms like Record.

When the company was listed in 2007 it came to the market on the back of very strong profitability that was still growing and was expected to continue. The company also had a suite of investment funds which invested in currencies and used leverage to increase potential returns.

These currency products were viewed as a separate asset class that could be sold to investors. But it is important to remember that currencies are quite volatile at the best of times. To add leverage to this volatile asset class can and did result in rather 'interesting' investment outcomes; not necessarily those which the investors in the currency products had hoped for.

It was not long before clients started to redeem these investments. Record, which had been a very profitable company on the back of these products, now started to suffer. In early 2008 the share price hit a high of 160p, but from then on it was on a relentless downward trajectory, hitting an all-time low of 9.75p in March 2012. This was when we spotted the company.

INVESTMENT CASE

We looked at the then-latest results for Record in March 2012 (released on 18 November 2011), where the interim results for the six months ended 30 September 2011. Record, despite its precipitous share-price fall, was still profitable and debt-free.

Looking at the balance sheet, current assets were £25,896,000 (of which cash and cash equivalents were £19,659,000!). Total liabilities only came to £4,336,000, leaving a net-net working capital position of £21,560,000 and a total of 220,796,714 shares in issue.

In this case the net-net working capital position (which was mainly made-up of cash) was 9.7p per share, compared to the then share price of 9.75p. Service companies like Record tend to be light on fixed assets; properties are leased, they have some intangibles, deferred tax assets etc. In this case the net asset value worked out at 10.4p. In other words, the fixed assets were only a small fraction of the total assets; the majority being made up of the current assets and, in particular, the cash position.

The following table gives some idea what the company had produced since it was listed in 2007.

	2007	2008	2009	2010	2011
Turnover (£m)	35.2	66.2	46.8	33.4	28.2
FRS3 pre-tax (£m)	19.6	40.4	26.8	16.6	12.5
ROCE (%)	132	225	98.5	66	43.2
FRS3 (EPS)	6.35	12.6	8.72	5.38	4.03

So in March 2012 the shares in Record could be bought at the net-net working capital position, while the business continued to be profitable, debt-free and paying a dividend.

The few analysts who still followed the company continued to focus on the ongoing downward trend in profitability, a result of the shrinking asset base (i.e. clients' funds) on which Record could charge a management fee. This was all undoubtedly true, but reading the results statement there were also some mildly positive comments in there:

"During the first six months there have been a number of changes in the sales team at record, including the recruitment of two senior individuals focussed on the US and Continental Europe respectively. This initiative, combined with the existing sales team, has positioned Record to focus on distribution of the expanded product range. It is anticipated that this focus should lead to additional mandates over the coming twelve months in both hedging and currency for return."

Shortly after having identified this company in March 2012 we decided to meet the management. This wasn't necessary – the investment case was already visible on paper – but it seemed a good idea. In this meeting it became clear that management had certainly not given up hope on a more rosy future. They saw plenty of opportunity to sell their services (if not their volatile currency products) to an ever-growing market.

As US pension funds continued to increase their foreign asset exposure there would come a point at which these funds would have to start considering hedging those exposures. It's a growing trend effecting the US pension fund and mutual fund industry in general. This is good news for Record. Not only are the international assets held by individual pension funds growing (which will result in Record receiving higher management fees), but the number of potential clients that need to have their currency exposure hedged is also growing.

Indeed, Record's salesman in charge of sales in continental Europe was mainly active in Switzerland, where they have a specific law that states that pension funds are obliged to have their foreign currency exposure fully hedged.

The main competition for Record's services are the banks, which for some years had been under pressure having suffered reputational damage, and where it was now seen as good management practice to employ different service providers to mitigate risk. This was another positive development for Record.

All this was not bad for a company which the stock market had basically given up on.

A CHANGING MODEL

Record's potential was still hidden behind the headline news of falling profitability and margin contraction. Why could no one see it? Was it a completely risk-free purchase?

Well, not quite. There were some potential downsides. It was certainly true that the new business opportunities that Record was beginning to focus on would attract far lower management charges. In the short term this would restrict a strong profit rebound, especially when compared to the previous peak profitability of 2007–8.

However, I would argue that the high profitability then produced was unsustainable due to the nature of the services offered. The new services may be less profitable but they have far greater durability; hedging, by its very nature, is a passive activity. The client relationship would be more stable. There would be much less scope for disappointment and acrimony, and much greater chance of long-term relationships – in, lest we forget, a market that had the potential to grow exponentially in the future.

The nature of the company's business was fundamentally changing. It used to be seen as an alternative fund manager, allocating assets upon which clients were looking for a return. This is a business model that carried a lot of risk. Just see how many of the previously high-flying publicly listed fund managers are now faring in the stock market.

Recent years have proved a difficult time for many of them and a number are now trading at fractions of their previous highs. (At some stage, when they can find a more endurable business model or when other things change, they may also become very interesting hunting grounds for deep value investors.)

Anyhow, Record's shift makes it a far safer business, allocating capital according to the service agreements with its clients, hedging their currency positions on a purely passive basis. This has the significant added value that volatility in the currency markets no longer directly affects Record, and the company is not reliant on trade activity (i.e. creating turnover) nor on calling the direction of currencies. This is very attractive – stockbroking companies, for instance, share many similarities with Record, but they are very reliant on the general state of the equity markets and the turnover that they can generate from that market, factors over which they have little direct control.

Having built this investment case, we bought shares in the company at 9.75p in March 2012.

OUTCOME

Since March 2012, Record has released several interim management statements that have hinted at more positive developments for the company. Client numbers are no longer falling; it has actually gained a few new ones. Management was also hopeful that further new clients would be signed-up before year-end 2013, and stated that they had been approached by potential new clients to discuss their service offering.

It is early days, but since the low in the share price of 9.75p in March 2012 the stock has started to appreciate, trading at 30p in November 2012. At the time of writing it was 34p.

I started this chapter by saying that the perfect value stock does not exist, but I think that this unique company comes very close to it. It shows high returns on capital, its business model is infinitely scalable, it has no balance sheet risk and it possesses a very big market to work on. The shares were bought when they seemed, in my eyes, to be priced in deep value territory. Hopefully with these new developments the company can return to 'normality' and will start attracting a wider following in the City.

This is not the type of investment which I will sell once net asset values (10.4p) have been breached. To do that I would have had to sell the stock a long time ago. This particular investment is too attractive for that. Once the market is convinced that profitability is stable and rising again, it will start focusing on these growing earnings. I have as yet no idea what profitability this company can reach, but if it can approach the 2010 level – generating earnings-per-share of 5.38p – then the current share price looks too low to me.

I bought it as a value stock and will sell when it has become an earnings story, hopefully at much higher levels.

EPILOGUE

I HOPE THAT THIS book has given you a better idea of what deep value investing entails. I have only concentrated on a very small area of the investing universe, but it seems to me one of the more rewarding.

Locating potential equity investments by seeking those trading at a discount to their net asset value, we tend to end up with many interesting opportunities. But as deep value investors we approach these from a different angle to the majority of equity investors. Unlike them we are not particularly interested in earnings or P/E levels. For us, a deep discount, liquid assets, a cyclical sector and a proven, nimble business model are the ideal. Earnings can be peanuts. In fact, shares going through a trough in their earnings are often ideal buys.

I hope I have shown that this approach can identify some genuinely worthwhile investments, and that when they work out (which they usually do) very good returns can be generated. A portfolio made up of these deep value investments can be a remarkably rewarding thing.

It is often said that this kind of equity investing must be quite risky. Unsurprisingly, I disagree! The companies may look distressed and be down in the doldrums. But we are largely purchasing liquid assets at a discount. It's like paying £20 for a £50 note. If these deep value stocks drop further after we've bought them, it usually means a chance to simply buy more for less – £50 for £10 or £5. The long term is what matters. And quality will out: either other investors will notice, or other companies will swoop in for a buyout.

Deep value investing is also safe because it is an incredibly restrained form of investment that means only investing when the potential upside is at its highest and risk is at its lowest. When only a few interesting value stocks can be found, it may well be that the market is at such a level that it is better to stay on the sidelines. The deep value investor does so cheerfully. It can take a lot of patience and may mean forgoing many seemingly attractive investments. But chasing earnings is one way to be sure of losing out when markets turn.

Instead, I try to be fully invested when the outlook is at its most worrisome, and head into cash and short-term high-quality bonds (gilts) as the markets become more confident. This may be lonely, but for anyone looking to really maximise their profits from the stock market it seems to me the only logical approach.

Just because the markets are open for trading, it does not mean that we have to trade. Buying stocks at objectively attractive prices means the market becomes our servant and not our master. Being a deep value investor means letting the market come to you.

ACKNOWLEDGEMENTS

The support of my wife, Anouk, has been invaluable, having suffered many years of living with a frustrated value investor before I could apply my ideas professionally at Church House Investments.

This book could not have been written but for the support that I have had from my colleagues at Church House Investments: James Mahon, Jeremy Wharton and Carol Hooper. Their continued encouragement and deep understanding of value investing made it for me a very easy environment in which to apply the value approach that we use for our investments.

Another big thank-you is due to Merryn Somerset Webb for not only reading a very early draft of this book but also for planting the idea to write it in the first place.